Colorado Mountain College
Spring Valley Learning Center
Glenwood Springs, CO 81601

Modern Critical Interpretations

The Gospels

Edited and with an introduction by

Harold Bloom
Sterling Professor of the Humanities
Yale University

Chelsea House Publishers ◊ *1988*
NEW YORK ◊ NEW HAVEN ◊ PHILADELPHIA

© 1988 by Chelsea House Publishers, a division
of Chelsea House Educational Communications, Inc.

Printed and bound in the United States of America

10 9 8 7 6 5 4 3 2 1

∞ The paper used in this publication meets the minimum
requirements of the American National Standard for Permanence
of Paper for Printed Library Materials, Z39.48-1984.

Library of Congress Cataloging-in-Publication Data
The Gospels.
    (Modern critical interpretations)
    Bibliography: p.
    Includes index.
    Contents: The way of Jesus / A.C. Charity—Jesus and
God / Hans Frei—A struggle with legion / Jean
Starobinski—The women at the tomb / Louis
Marin—[etc.]
    1. Bible. N.T. Gospels—Criticism, interpretation,
etc.   2. Bible as literature.   I. Bloom, Harold.
II. Series.
BS2555.2.G624   1988   226'.066   87-24222
ISBN 0-87754-911-7 (alk. paper)

Contents

Editor's Note

This book gathers together what I judge to be the best modern *literary* critical interpretations of the Gospels. The essays are reprinted here in the order of their original publication. I am grateful to Brandon Lawrence and Frank Menchaca for their assistance in editing this volume.

My introduction, somewhat polemical in its stance, seeks to define the agonistic position taken up by the Gospel of John in regard to the Hebrew Bible and to the figure of Moses in particular. The chronological sequence of criticism begins with A. C. Charity, who gives a typological reading of Jesus in the Gospels as being the "Way" or fulfillment of the path of Israel.

Hans Frei, studying the representation of Jesus in Gospel narrative, explores the limit set upon theology by the shape of the narrative. In a reading of Mark 5:1–20, Jean Starobinski meditates upon the casting out of the demon so suggestively called "Legion." Louis Marin subjects the Gospel accounts of the women at the tomb of Jesus to a structural analysis, while Frank Kermode broods upon the obscurity of the Gospel parables that both proclaim and conceal their messages.

We return to literary typology with Northrop Frye's exegesis of the intensification of prophecy in the Gospels. In a very different critical mode Elisabeth Schüssler Fiorenza studies the women disciples of Jesus as paradigms for all true discipleship, male and female.

The belatedness of the Fourth Gospel, examined in my introduction in relation to the Hebrew Bible, is examined in regard to the three earlier Gospels by Donald Foster. René Girard concludes this volume by his analysis of Peter's denial of Jesus, which Girard insists is in no way rightly understood by the narrators of the Gospels.

Introduction

> "Your father Abraham rejoiced that he was to see my
> days; he saw it and was glad." The Jews then said to him,
> "You are not yet fifty years old, and have you seen Abra-
> ham?" Jesus said to them, "Truly, truly, I say to you, before
> Abraham was, I am."
>
> (John 8:56–58)

This exchange from the Gospel according to St. John will be my text.
In the Christian triumph over the Hebrew Bible, a triumph which
produced that captive work, the Old Testament, there is no more
heroic stroke than the transumptive trope of John's Jesus: "Before
Abraham was, I am." Too much is carried by that figuration for any
range of readings to convey, but one reading I shall give is the implied
substitution: "Before Moses was, I am." To my reading, the author of
the Gospel of John was and is a more dangerous enemy of the Hebrew
Bible than even Paul, his nearest rival. But I can hardly go on until I
explain what I intend to mean by "an enemy of the Hebrew Bible."

It is now altogether too late in Western history for pious or humane
self-deceptions on the matter of the Christian appropriation of the
Hebrew Bible. It is certainly much too late in Jewish history to be
other than totally clear about the nature and effect of that Christian act
of total usurpation. The best preliminary description I have found is
by Jaroslav Pelikan:

> What the Christian tradition had done was to take over the
> Jewish Scriptures as its own, so that Justin could say to

1

Trypho that the passages about Christ "are contained in your Scriptures, or rather not yours, but ours." As a matter of fact, some of the passages were contained only in "ours," that is, in the Christian Old Testament. So assured were Christian theologians in their possession of the Scriptures that they could accuse the Jews not merely of misunderstanding and misinterpreting them, but even of falsifying scriptural texts. When they were aware of differences between the Hebrew text of the Old Testament and the Septuagint, they capitalized on these to prove their accusation. . . . The growing ease with which appropriations and accusations alike could be made was in proportion to the completeness of the Christian victory over Jewish thought.

Yet that victory was achieved largely by default. Not the superior force of Christian exegesis or learning or logic but the movement of Jewish history seems to have been largely responsible for it.

Pelikan's dispassionate judgment on this matter is beyond disputation. Though the Christians were to "save" the Old Testament from those like Marcion who would cast it out completely, that is precisely what they saved—*their* Old Testament. The New Testament is to a considerable extent a reading of that Old Testament, and I would judge it a very mixed reading indeed. Some of it is a strong misreading, and much of it is a weak misreading, but I will concern myself here entirely with strong misreadings, because only strong misreadings work so as to establish lasting enmities between texts. The author of the Gospel of John is an even stronger misreader than St. Paul, and I want to compare John's and Paul's strengths of what I call poetic misprision before I center upon John. But before commencing, I had better declare my own stance.

"Who is the interpreter, and what power does he seek to gain over the text?" That Nietzschean question haunts me always. I am an enemy of the New Testament. My enmity is lifelong, and intensifies as I study its text more closely. But I have no right to assert that my own enmity carries the force of the normative Jewish tradition, because I am not a representative of that tradition. From a normative Jewish perspective, let us say from the stance of the great Akiba, I am one of the *minim,* the Jewish Gnostic heretics. My own reading of the Hebrew

Bible, even if I develop it into a strong misreading, is as unacceptable in its way to the normative tradition as all Christian readings necessarily are. I state this not to posture, but to make clear that I do not pretend to the authority of the normative tradition. In my view, the Judaism that moves in a continuous line from the Academy of Ezra through the Pharisees and on to the religion of my own parents is itself a very powerful misreading of the Hebrew Bible and so of the religion of the Yahwist, whatever we might take that religion to have been. But my subject here is not the text of the Yahwist.

What kind of authority can a literary critic, whose subject is the secular literature of the English language, bring to a reading of the New Testament, particularly to a reading that sees the New Testament as a text in conflict and confrontation with the Hebrew Bible? I cannot speak for other literary critics, as here too I am a sect or party of one, and have no authority other than whatever my ideas and my writings can assert for me. But the central concern of my own literary theory and praxis, for some fifteen years now, has been the crisis of confrontation and conflict between what I have called strong poems, or strong texts. I cannot say that my formulations in this area have met with a very amiable reception, even in the most secular of contexts, and so I do not expect an amiable response as I cross the line into the conflict of scriptures. Still, I have learned a great deal from the response to my work, a response that necessarily has become part of my subject. One lesson has been that there are no purely secular texts, because canonization of poems by the secular academies is not merely a displaced version of Jewish or Christian or Moslem canonization. It is precisely the thing itself, the investment of a text with unity, presence, form, and meaning, followed by the insistence that the canonized text possesses these attributes immutably, quite apart from the interpretive activities of the academies.

If so many partisans of Wordsworth or Whitman or Stevens find the offense of my work unbearable, then clearly I must expect a yet more pained response from the various custodians of the Hebrew Bible or the New Testament. I won't take more space here for unhappy anticipation or personal defense, yet I do want to make the modest observation that several years spent intensely in reading as widely as I can in biblical scholarship have not left me with the impression that much authentic *literary* criticism of biblical texts has been written. To make a clean sweep of it, little seems to me to have been added by recent overt intercessions by literary critics, culminating in Northrop Frye's *The Great Code*, a work in which the triumph of the New Testament over the Hebrew Bible is quite flatly complete. Frye's code, like Erich Auerbach's *figura*, which I have attacked elsewhere, is only another belated repetition of the Christian appropriation and usurpation of the Hebrew Bible.

But these matters I will argue elsewhere. I come back again to the grand proclamation of John's Jesus: "Before Abraham was, I am." What can an antithetical literary criticism (as I call my work) do with the sublime force of that assertion? Or how should that force be described? It is not the New Testament's antithetical reply to the Yahwist's most sublime moment, when Moses agonizingly stammers: "If I come to the people of Israel and say to them, 'The God of your fathers has sent me to you,' and they ask me, 'What is his name?' what shall I say to them?" God said to Moses, "I AM WHO I AM." This is the Revised Standard Version, and like every other version, it cannot handle Yahweh's awesome, untranslatable play upon his own name: *ehyeh asher ehyeh*. I expand upon a suggestion of Martin Buber's when I render this as "I will be present wherever and whenever I will be present." For that is the Yahwist's vision of *olam* as "a time without boundaries," and of the relation of Yahweh to a dynamics of time that transcends spatial limitations.

The Yahwist's vision of his God certainly would seem to center with a peculiar intensity upon the text of Exodus 3:13–14. But the entire history of ancient Jewish exegesis hardly would lead anyone to believe that this crucial passage was of the slightest interest or importance to any of the great rabbinical commentators. The *Exodus Rabbah* offers mostly midrashim connecting the name of God to his potencies which would deliver Israel from Egypt. But *ehyeh asher ehyeh* as a phrase evidently did not have peculiar force for the great Pharisees. Indeed, Jewish tradition does very little with the majestic proclamation until Maimonides gets to work upon it in *The Guide for the Perplexed*. One of my favorite books, Marmorstein's fascinating *The Old Rabbinic Doctrine of God*, has absolutely not a single reference to Exodus 3 in its exhaustive one-hundred-fifty-page section on "The Names of God." Either we must conclude that *ehyeh asher ehyeh* has very little significance for Akiba and his colleagues, which I think probably was the case, or we must resort to dubious theories of taboo, which have little to do with the strength of Akiba.

This puzzle becomes greater when the early rabbinical indifference to the striking *ehyeh asher ehyeh* text is contrasted to the Christian obsession with Exodus 3, which begins in the New Testament and becomes overwhelming in the church fathers, culminating in Augustine's endless preoccupation with that passage, since for Augustine it was the deepest clue to the metaphysical essence of God. Brevard Childs, in his commentary on Exodus, has outlined the history of this long episode in Christian exegesis. Respectfully, I dissent from his judgment that the ontological aspects of Christian interpretation here really do have any continuity whatsoever either with the biblical text or with rabbinical traditions. These "ontological overtones," as Childs himself has to note, stem rather from the Septuagint's rendering of *ehyeh asher ehyeh* as the very different ἐγώ εἰμι ὁ ὤν and from Philo's very Platonized paraphrase in his *Life of Moses:* "Tell them that I am He Who is, that they may learn the difference between what is and what is not." Though Childs insists that this cannot be dismissed as Greek thinking, it is nothing but that, and explains again why Philo was so crucial for Christian theology and so totally irrelevant to the continuity of normative Judaism.

The continued puzzle, then, is the total lack of early rabbinical interest in the *ehyeh asher ehyeh* text. I labor this point because I read John's greatest subversion of the Hebrew Bible as what I call this transumption of Yahweh's words to Moses in that extraordinary outburst of John's Jesus, "Before Abraham was, I am," which most deeply proclaims: "Before Moses was, I am." To me, this is the acutest manifestation of John's palpable ambivalence toward Moses, an ambivalence whose most perceptive student has been Wayne Meeks. John plays on and against the Yahwist's grand wordplay on Yahweh, and *ehyeh.* However, when I assert even that, I go against the authority of the leading current scholarly commentary upon the Fourth Gospel, and so I must deal with this difficulty before I return to the Johannic ambivalence toward the Moses traditions. And only after examining John's agon with Moses will I feel free to speculate upon the early rabbinic indifference to God's substitution of *ehyeh asher ehyeh* for his proper name.

Both B. Lindars and C. K. Barrett in their standard commentaries on John insist that "Before Abraham was, I am" makes no allusion whatsoever to "I am that I am." A literary critic must begin by observing that New Testament scholarship manifests a very impoverished notion as to just what literary allusion is or can be. But then here is Barrett's flat reading of this assertion of Jesus: "The meaning here is: Before Abraham came into being, I eternally was, as now I am, and ever continue to be." Perhaps I should not chide devoted scholars like Lindars and Barrett for being inadequate interpreters of so extraordinary a trope, because the master modern interpreter of John, Rudolf Bultmann, seems to me even less capable of handling trope. Here is his reading of John 8:57–58:

> The Jews remain caught in the trammels of their own thought. How can Jesus, who is not yet 50 years old, have seen Abraham! Yet the world's conception of time and age is worthless, when it has to deal with God's revelation, as is its conception of life and death. "Before Abraham was, I am." The Revealer, unlike Abraham, does not belong to the ranks of historical personages. The ἐγώ which Jesus speaks as the Revealer is the "I" of the eternal Logos, which was in the beginning, the "I" of the eternal God himself. Yet the Jews cannot comprehend that the ἐγώ of eternity is to be heard in an historical person, who is not yet 50 years old, who as a man is one of their equals, whose mother and father they knew. They cannot understand, because the notion of the Revealer's "pre-existence" can only be understood in faith.

In a note, Bultmann too denies any allusion to the "I am that I am" declaration of Yahweh. I find it ironical, nearly two thousand years after St. Paul accused the Jews of being literalizers, that the leading scholars of Christianity are hopeless literalizers, which of course the great rabbis never were. I cannot conceive of a weaker misreading of "Before Abraham was, I am" than Bultmann's sneering retreat into "faith," a "faith" in the "pre-existence" of Jesus. If that is all John meant, then John was a weak poet indeed. But John is at his best here, and at his best he is a strong misreader and thus a strong writer. As for Bultmann's polemical point, I am content to repeat a few amiable remarks made by Rabbi David Kimhi almost eight hundred years ago:

> Tell them that there can be no father and son in the Divinity, for the Divinity is indivisible and is one in every aspect of unity unlike matter which is divisible.
>
> Tell them further that a father precedes a son in time and a son is born through the agency of a father. Now even though each of the terms "father" and "son" implies the other . . . he who is called the father must undoubtedly be prior in time. Therefore, with reference to this God whom

you call Father, Son, and Holy Spirit, that part which you
call Father must be prior to that which you call Son, for if
they were always coexistent, they would have to be called
twin brothers.

I have cited this partly because I enjoy it so much, but also because
it raises the true issue between Moses and John, between Abraham and
Jesus, which is the agonistic triple issue of priority, authority, and
originality. As I read John's trope, it asserts not only the priority of
Jesus over Abraham (and so necessarily over Moses), but also the
priority, authority, and originality of John over Moses, or as we
would say, of John as writer over the Yahwist as writer. That is where
I am heading this account of the agon between the Yahwist and John,
and so I turn now to some general observations upon the Fourth
Gospel—observations by a literary critic, of course, and not by a
qualified New Testament believer and/or scholar.

John does seem to me the most anxious in tone of all the gospels,
and its anxiety is as much what I would call a literary anxiety as an
existential or spiritual one. One sign of this anxiety is the palpable
difference between the attitude of Jesus toward himself in the Fourth
Gospel as compared to the other three. Scholarly consensus holds that
John was written at the close of the first century, and so after the
synoptic Gospels. A century is certainly enough time for apocalyptic
hope to have ebbed away, and for an acute sense of belatedness to have
developed in its place. John's Jesus has a certain obsession with his own
glory, and particularly with what that glory ought to be in a Jewish
context. Rather like the Jesus of Gnosticism, John's Jesus is much
given to saying "I am," and there are Gnostic touches throughout
John, though their extent is disputable. Perhaps, as some scholars have
surmised, there is an earlier, more Gnostic gospel buried in the Gospel
of John. An interesting article by John Meagher of Toronto, back in
1969, even suggested that the original reading of John 1:14 was "And
the Word became *pneuma* and dwelt among us," which is a Gnostic
formulation, yet curiously more in the spirit and tone of much of the
Fourth Gospel than is "And the Word became flesh."

The plain nastiness of the Gospel of John toward the Pharisees is
in the end an anxiety as to the spiritual authority of the Pharisees, and
it may be augmented by John's Gnostic overtones. A Jewish reader
with even the slightest sense of Jewish history, feels threatened when
reading John 18:28–19:16. I do not think that this feeling has anything

to do with the supposed pathos or problematic literary power of the text. There is a peculiar wrongness about John's Jesus saying, "If my kingship were of this world, my servants would fight, that I might not be handed over to the Jews" (18:36); it implies that Jesus is no longer a Jew, but something else. This unhappy touch is another sign of the pervasive rhetoric of anxiety in the Fourth Gospel. John's vision seemed to be of a small group—his own, presumably—which finds its analogue and asserted origin in the group around Jesus two generations before. In the general judgment of scholars, the original conclusion of the gospel was the parable of doubting Thomas, a manifest trope for a sect or coven undergoing a crisis of faith.

It is within that anxiety of frustrate expectations, perhaps even of recent expulsion from the Jewish world, that John's agon with Moses finds its context. Wayne Meeks has written very sensitively of the Fourth Gospel's ambivalence toward the Moses traditions, particularly those centered upon the image of Moses as prophet-king, a unique amalgam of the two roles that John seeks to extend and surpass in Jesus. My interest in John's handling of Moses is necessarily different in emphasis, for I am going to read a number of John's namings of Moses as being tropes more for the text than for the supposed substance of what the New Testament (following the Septuagint) insists upon calling the Law. I myself will call it not Torah but J or the Yahwist, because that is where I locate the agon. Not theology, not faith, not truth is the issue, but literary power, the scandalous power of J's text, which by synecdoche stands for the Hebrew Bible as the strongest poem that I have ever read in any language I am able to read. John, and Paul before him, took on an impossible precursor and rival, and their apparent victory is merely an illusion. The aesthetic dignity of the Hebrew Bible, and of the Yahwist in particular as its uncanny original, is simply beyond the competitive range of the New Testament as a literary achievement, as it is beyond the range of the only surviving Gnostic texts that have any aesthetic value—a few fragments of Valentinus and the Gospel of Truth that Valentinus may have written. But I will return to the end of this discourse to the issue of rival aesthetic achievements. John's struggle with Moses is at last my direct concern.

There are so many contests with Moses throughout the New Testament that I cannot contrast John in this regard to all of the other texts, but I do want to compare him briefly with Paul, if only because I intend later to consider some aspects of Paul's own struggle with the

Hebrew Bible. I think there is still nothing so pungent in all commentary upon Paul as the remarks made by Nietzsche in 1888, in *The Antichrist:*

> Paul is the incarnation of a type which is the reverse of that of the Savior; he is the genius in hatred, in the standpoint of hatred, and in the relentless logic of hatred. . . . What he wanted was power; with St. Paul the priest again aspired to power,—he could make use only of concepts, doctrines, symbols with which masses may be tyrannised over, and with which herds are formed.

Of course Nietzsche is extreme, but can he be refuted? Paul is so careless, hasty, and inattentive a reader of the Hebrew Bible that he very rarely gets any text right; and in so gifted a person this kind of weak misunderstanding can come only from the dialectics of the power drive, of the will to power over a text, even when the text is as formidable as Torah. There is little agonistic cunning in Paul's misreadings of Torah; many indeed are plain howlers. The most celebrated is his weird exegesis of Exodus 34:29–35, where the text has Moses descending from Sinai, tablets in hand, his face shining with God's glory—a glory so great that Moses must veil his countenance after speaking to the people, and then unveil only when he returns to speak to God. Normative Jewish interpretation, surely known to Paul, was that the shining was the Torah restoration of the *zelem*, the true image of God that Adam had lost, and that the shining prevailed until the death of Moses. But here is 2 Corinthians 3:12-13:

> Since we have such a hope, we are very bold, not like Moses, who put a veil over his face so that the Israelites might not see the end of the fading splendor.

There isn't any way to save this, even by gently calling it a "parody" of the Hebrew text, as Wayne Meeks does. It isn't a transumption or lie against time, which is the Johannine mode; it is just a plain lie against the text. Nor is it uncharacteristic of Paul. Meeks very movingly calls Paul "the Christian Proteus," and Paul is certainly beyond my understanding. Proteus is an apt model for many other roles, but perhaps not for an interpreter of Mosaic text. Paul's reading of what he thought was the Law increasingly seems to me oddly Freudian, in that Paul identifies the Law with the human drive that Freud wanted to call Thanatos. Paul's peculiar confounding of the Law and death presumably keeps him from seeing Jesus as a transcending fulfillment of Moses. Instead, Paul contrasts himself to Moses, hardly to his own disadvantage. Thus, Romans 9:3:

> For I could wish that I myself were accused and cut off from
> Christ for the sake of my brethren, my kinsmen by race.

It may seem at first an outburst of Jewish pride, of which I would grant the Protean Paul an authentic share, but the Mosaic allusion changes its nature. All exegetes point to Exodus 32:32 as the precursor text. Moses offers himself to Yahweh as atonement for the people after the orgy of the golden calf: "But now, if thou wilt forgive their sin—and if not, blot me, I pray thee, out of thy book which thou hast written." How do the two offers of intercession compare? After all, the people *have* sinned, and Moses would choose oblivion to save them from the consequences of their disloyalty. The allusive force of Paul's offer is turned against both his own Jewish contemporaries and even against Moses himself. Even the Pharisees (for whom Paul, unlike John, has a lingering regard) are worshippers of the golden calf of death, since the Law *is* death. And all Moses supposedly offered was the loss of his own prophetic greatness, his place in the salvation history. But Paul, out of supposed love for his fellow-Jews, offers to lose more than Moses did, because he insists he has more to lose. To be cut off from Christ is to die eternally, a greater sacrifice than the Mosaic offer to be as one who had never lived. This is what I would call the daemonic counter-Sublime of hyperbole, and its repressive force is enormous and very revelatory.

But I return again to John, whose revisionary warfare against Moses is subtler. Meeks has traced the general pattern, and so I follow him here, though of course he would dissent from the interpretation I am going to offer of this pattern of allusion. The allusions begin with John the Baptist chanting a typical Johannine metalepsis, in which the latecomer truly has priority ("John bore witness to him, and cried, 'This was he of whom I said: He who comes after me ranks before me, for he was before me' "), to which the author of the Fourth Gospel adds: "For the law was given through Moses; grace and truth came through Jesus Christ" (John 1:15, 17). Later, the first chapter proclaims: "We have found him of whom Moses in the law and also the prophets wrote, Jesus of Nazareth" (1:45). The third chapter daringly inverts a great Mosaic trope in a way still unnerving for any Jewish reader: "No one has ascended into heaven but he who descended from heaven, the Son of man. And as Moses lifted up the serpent in the wilderness, so must the Son of man be lifted up" (3:13–14). John's undoubted revisionary genius is very impressive here merely from a technical or rhetorical point of view. No heavenly revelations ever were made to Moses, whose function is reduced to a synecdoche, and indeed to its lesser half. To use one of my revisionary ratios, Jesus on the cross will be the *tessera* or antithetical completion of the Mosaic raising of the brazen serpent in the wilderness. Moses was only a part, but Jesus is the fulfilling whole. My avoidance of the language of typology, here and elsewhere, is quite deliberate, and will be defended in my conclusion, where I will say a few unkind words about the Christian and now Auerbachian trope of *figura*.

The same ratio of antithetical completion is invoked when Jesus announces himself as the fulfiller of the sign of manna, as would be expected of the Messiah. But here the gratuitous ambivalence toward Moses is sharper: "Truly, truly, I say to you, it was not Moses who gave you the bread from heaven; my Father gives you the true bread from heaven. For the bread of God is that which comes down from heaven, and gives life to the world" (6:32–33). As the trope is developed, it becomes deliberately so shocking in a Jewish context that even the disciples are shocked; but I would point to one moment in the development as marking John's increasing violence against Moses and all the Jews: "Your fathers ate the manna in the wilderness, and they died. . . . I am the living bread . . . if any one eats of this bread, he will live for ever; and the bread which I shall give for the life of the world is my flesh" (6:49, 51). It is, after all, gratuitous to say that our fathers ate the manna and died; it is even misleading, since had they not eaten the manna, they would not have lived as long as they did. But John has modulated to a daemonic counter-Sublime, and his hyperbole helps to establish a new, Christian sublimity, in which Jews die and Christians live eternally.

Rather than multiply instances of John's revisionism, I want to conclude my specific remarks on the Fourth Gospel by examining in its full context the passage with which I began: "Before Abraham was, I am." I am more than a little unhappy with the sequence I will expound, because I find in it John at nearly his most unpleasant and indeed anti-Jewish, but the remarkable rhetorical strength of "Before Abraham was, I am" largely depends upon its contextualization, as John undoes the Jewish pride in being descended from Abraham. The sequence, extending through most of the eighth chapter, begins with Jesus sitting in the temple, surrounded both by Pharisees and by Jews who are in the process of becoming his believers. To those he has begun to persuade, Jesus now says what is certain to turn them away:

> "If you continue in my word, you are truly my disciples, and you will know the truth, and the truth will make you free." They answered him, "We are descendants of Abraham, and have never been in bondage to any one. How is it that you say, 'You will be made free'?"
>
> (8:31–32)

It seems rather rhetorically weak that Jesus should then become aggressive, with a leap into murderous insinuations:

> "I know that you are descendants of Abraham; yet you seek to kill me, because my word finds no place in you. I speak of what I have seen with my Father, and you do what you have heard from your father."
>
> (8:37–38)

As John's Jesus graciously is about to tell them, the Jews' father is the devil. They scarcely can be blamed for answering, "Abraham is our father," or for assuming that their accuser has a demon. I look at the foot of the page of the text I am using, *The New Oxford Annotated Bible, Revised Standard Version* (1977), and next to verse 48, on having a demon, the editors helpfully tell me, "*The Jews* turn to insult and calumny." I reflect upon how wonderful a discipline such scholarship is, and I mildly rejoin that by any dispassionate reading John's Jesus has made the initial "turn to insult and calumny." What matter, since the Jews are falling neatly into John's rhetorical trap? Jesus has promised that his believers "will never see death" and the astonished children of Abraham (or is it children of the devil?) protest:

> "Abraham died, as did the prophets; and you say, 'If any one keeps my word, he will never taste death.' Are you greater than our father Abraham, who died?"
>
> (8:52–53)

Jesus responds by calling them liars, again surely rather gratuitously, and then by ensnaring them in John's subtlest tropological entrapment, which will bring me full circle to where I began:

> "Your father Abraham rejoiced that he was to see my day; he saw it and was glad." The Jews then said to him,

"You are not yet fifty years old, and have you seen Abraham?" Jesus said to them, "Truly, truly, I say to you, before Abraham was, I am."

(8:57–58)

It is certainly the most remarkable transumption in the New Testament, though I had better explain what I mean by transumption, which is a little exhausting for me, since I have been explaining the term endlessly in eight books published over the last nine years. Very briefly, transumption or metalepsis is the traditional term in rhetoric for the trope that works to make the late seem early, and the early seem late. It lies against time, so as to accomplish what Nietzsche called the will's revenge against time, and against time's assertion, "It was." Uniquely among figures of speech, transumption works to undo or reverse anterior tropes. It is therefore the particular figure that governs what we might call "interpretive allusion." Ultimately, it seeks to end stop allusiveness by presenting its own formulation as the last word, which insists upon an ellipsis rather than a proliferation of further allusion.

When John's Jesus says, "Before Abraham was, I am," the ultimate allusion is not to Abraham but to Moses, and to Yahweh's declaration made to Moses, "I am that I am." The transumption leaps over Abraham by saying also, "Before Moses was, I am," and by hinting ultimately: "I am that I am"—because I am one with my father Yahweh. The ambivalence and agonistic intensity of the Fourth Gospel achieves an apotheosis with this sublime introjection of Yahweh, which simultaneously also is a projection or repudiation of Abraham and Moses. I am aware that I seem to be making John into a Gnostic Christian, but that is the transumptive force of his rhetoric, as opposed perhaps to his more overt dialectic. His Gospel, as it develops, does seem to me to become as Gnostic as it is Christian, and this is the kind of Gnosticism that indeed was a kind of intellectual or spiritual anti-Semitism. Obviously, I believe that there are Gnosticisms and Gnosticisms, and some I find considerably more attractive than others. Just as obviously, the Gnostic elements in John, and even in St. Paul, seem to me very shadowed indeed.

Earlier in this discourse, I confessed my surprise at the normative rabbinical indifference, in ancient days, to Yahweh's sublime declaration, *ehyeh asher ehyeh*. If the great Rabbi Akiba ever speculated about that enigmatic phrase, he kept it to himself. I doubt that he made any such speculations, because I do not think that fearless sage was in the habit of hoarding them, and I am not enough of a Kabbalist to think that Akiba harbored forbidden or esoteric knowledge. To the normative mind of the Judaism roughly contemporary with Jesus, there was evidently nothing remarkable in Yahweh's declining to give his name, and instead almost playfully asserting: "Tell them that I who will be when and where I will be am the one who has sent you." That is how Yahweh talked, and how he was. But to the belated author of the Fourth Gospel, as to all our belated selves, "I am that I am" was and is a kind of *mysterium tremendum,* to use Rudolf Otto's language. That mystery John sought to transcend and transume with the formulation "Before Abraham was, I am." Prior to the text of Exodus was the text that John was writing, in which the Jews were to be swept away into the universe of death, while Jesus led John on to the universe of life.

This transformation is an instance of just how the New Testament reduced the Hebrew Bible to that captive work, the Old Testament. Though the reduction is necessarily of great theological influence, it of course does not touch the Hebrew Bible. I have read the Hebrew Bible since I was a child, and the New Testament since I first took a course in New Testament Greek as an undergraduate. Clearly, I am not a dispassionate reader of the New Testament, though I do not read the Hebrew Bible as the normative Jewish tradition had read it, either. I come back to the issue of the interpreter's authority. When I read, I read as a literary critic, but my concerns have little in common with those of any contemporary critic. Idealizations of any text, however canonical, or of the reading process itself are not much to my taste. Emerson said he read for the lustres. I follow him, but I emphasize even more that the lustres arise out of strife, competition, defense, anxiety, and the author's constant need for survival *as an author.* I don't see how any authentic literary critic could judge John as anything better than a very flawed revisionist of the Yahwist, and Paul as something less than that, despite the peculiar pathos of his protean personality. In the aesthetic warfare between the Hebrew Bible and the New Testament, there is just no contest, and if you think otherwise, then bless you.

But surely the issue is not aesthetic, I will be reminded. Well, we are all trapped in history, and the historical triumph of Christianity is brute fact. I am not moved to say anything about it. But I am moved to reject the idealized modes of interpretation it has stimulated, from early typology on to the revival of *figura* by Erich Auerbach and the

Blakean Great Code of Northrop Frye. No text, secular or religious, fulfills another text, and all who insist otherwise merely homogenize literature. As for the relevance of the aesthetic to the issue of the conflict between sacred texts, I doubt finally that much else is relevant to a strong reader who is not dominated by extraliterary persuasions or convictions. Reading *The Book of Mormon*, for instance, is a difficult aesthetic experience, and I would grant that not much in the New Testament subjects me to rigors of quite that range. But then John and Paul do not ask to be read against *The Book of Mormon*.

Can the New Testament be read as less polemically and destructively revisionary of the Hebrew Bible than it actually is? Not by me, anyway. But don't be too quick to shrug off a reading informed by an awareness of the ways of the antithetical, of the revisionary strategies devised by those latecomers who seek strength, and who will sacrifice truth to get strength even as they proclaim the incarnation of the truth beyond death. Nietzsche is hardly the favorite sage of contemporary New Testament scholars, but perhaps he still has something vital to teach them.

What do Jews and Christians gain by refusing to see that the revisionary desperation of the New Testament has made it permanently impossible to identify the Hebrew Bible with the Christian Old Testament? Doubtless there are social and political benefits in idealizations of "dialogue," but there is nothing more. It is not a contribution to the life of the spirit or the intellect to tell lies to one another or to oneself in order to bring about more affection or cooperation between Christians and Jews. Paul is hopelessly equivocal on nearly every subject, but to my reading he is clearly not a Jewish anti-Semite; yet his misrepresentation of Torah was absolute. John is evidently a Jewish anti-Semite, and the Fourth Gospel is pragmatically murderous as an anti-Jewish text. Yet it is theologically and emotionally central to Christianity. I give the last word to the sage called Radak in Jewish tradition, that David Kimhi whom I cited earlier. He quotes as proof text Ezekiel 16:53: "I will turn their captivity, the captivity of Sodom and her daughters." And then Radak comments, rightly dismissing from his perspective all Christians as mere heretics from Judaism: "This verse is a reply to the Christian heretics who say that the future consolations have already been fulfilled. *Sodom is still overturned as it was and is still unsettled.*"

The Way of Jesus

A. C. Charity

"Christianity [as M. Burrows writes in *More Light on the Dead Sea Scrolls*], arose within Judaism and was first offered to Jews by Jews as the true Judaism, not as replacing but as fulfilling the faith of their fathers. This faith, whether expressed in law, discourse, prediction, or historiography, amounted above all to a confession that God worked in and through history, that in history certain "mighty acts" were more or less directly ascribable to him, and that man's existence stood totally in dependence upon God and the activity of God.

So that if Jesus offered himself or was to be offered to Jews as the fulfilment of this history he must show himself or be shown as doing something essentially comparable and related to the decisive works of God in the Old Testament. It is not only a matter of fulfilling the promises made to Abraham, Moses, and all the prophets, though that too Paul claimed that Jesus had done: "He is the Yes pronounced upon God's promises, every one of them" (2 Cor. 1:20). It is also a matter of showing that, despite the apparent unlikeliness, the obscure rabbi who set about preaching in Galilee and continued upon his way up to Jerusalem to be hanged as a criminal, did this, as he claimed, in fulfilment of a requirement already laid down in the Scriptures: "The Son of Man is going the way appointed for him in the Scriptures" (Mark 14:21).

Now without denying that this kind of statement, which occurs

From *Events and Their Afterlife: The Dialectics of Christian Typology in the Bible and Dante*. © 1966 by Cambridge University Press.

fairly frequently in the Gospels, is still, as it was to Jesus' contemporaries, enigmatic, and apparently deliberately so, I believe that we can in the light of biblical scholarship make several points about its significance with some certainty. First, that the metaphor of the "way" probably goes back to Jesus himself, and is in any case a primary category for the explanation and understanding of Jesus' earthly mission and work. Secondly, that (despite popular impressions) the form of this "way" is appointed not only in the predictions of the Old Testament and in the expectations of later Judaism, but also, and mainly, in something less specific and more fundamental to the Old Testament message, namely, the Old Testament's general understanding of Israel's election and calling. And thirdly, that when we (and Jesus and the New Testament writers) apply the idea of "fulfilment" to this concept of an appointed way and locate this fulfilment in Jesus' mission we are making a claim that is incomprehensible except in terms of typology, namely, that Jesus "recapitulates"—i.e., repeats and fulfills—the historical existence of Israel.

The first of these points may be substantiated only sketchily here. For a fuller treatment I must refer once again to the work of E. J. Tinsley, upon whose discussion I here mainly depend. To begin with, the fact that the Christian religion was first known as "the Way" (Acts 9:2; 16:17; 18:25, etc.) already suggests a high degree of probability that the term goes back, almost as a *terminus technicus*, to the teaching of Jesus, who was himself, as John saw, "the Way" (John 14:6). The same image and significance is present in the phrase "follow me." By thus personifying "the Way" in the person of Jesus the early Christians mean not only that he "teaches the way of God" (Mark 11:14, where the way of God is the law, as the continuation makes plain) but primarily that it is through him that one may have access to God (cf. again John 14:6, especially "no one comes to the Father except by me"; also Heb. 10:20). Yet the precondition for Jesus to "be the Way" must be that he himself "goes on the way." The image which Luke develops at length in his long central narrative of the journey to Jerusalem (Luke 9:51–19:44)—a journey which is determined, not only by Jesus (9:51), but also by Scripture (18:31; 13:33)—has a secure place too in Matthew and Mark, where once again it is accompanied by the notes of compulsion and foreordination (e.g., Mark 10:32 ff.; 14:21; Matt. 16:21).

It will be noticed that of these instances (e.g., Mark 10:33; 14:21) are associated with the term "Son of Man" and with suffering and death. The extent to which these ideas are themselves typological will be discussed later; in the meantime we must note that, while the Passion is conceived as the end of Jesus' mission, the mission begins with the narratives of baptism and temptation, and these narratives, too, are linked with the idea of a "way." The beginning of Mark is a case in point, where the prophecies in Malachi 3:1 and Isaiah 40:3, both of which refer to the preparation of a way, are brought together to explain the coming of John the Baptist. The inference is clear: John is to prepare the way, but Jesus will walk in it. Although in a certain sense verses 2–3 suggest the fulfilment of prophecy they still offer a prophecy whose fulfilment at that stage had not come about, they still look forward to an event of fulfilment proper. It is only with verse 15, in the preaching of Jesus, that this time shift is said to have happened: "The time is fulfilled, and the Kingdom of God has drawn near." Thus "the way of the Lord" is initiated, and it is initiated, significantly, with Jesus' baptism and the temptation "in the wilderness."

We have noticed the frequent parallelism in the Old Testament between *derek* (way) and *torah* (law). Obedience to the commandments meant "following after" God who had led Israel on the way through the wilderness. "In the Book of Deuteronomy there is a continual oscillation between *derek* meaning the actual historical way which Israel has traversed from Red Sea to Promised Land, and *derek* meaning the 'way of life' to which the people are consequently summoned. . . . The image of the 'Way' is never detached from the historical journey once taken." Much nearer New Testament times the same alternation between the two contexts of *derek* is to be found in the "Dead Sea Scrolls." The Qumran community, indeed, made the synthesis closer even than it was in the orthodox *cultus*. They thought of their mission and existence as "the perfect way" which they traversed in the wilderness to "prepare the way of the Lord" (Isa. 40:3). The verse from Isaiah is quoted in the *Manual of Discipline* (8:12–14) and applied to their own situation both as explaining their presence in the desert and as implying the duty of studying the law. "When the (Covenanters) first established themselves in the Wilderness of Judaea, they predicted a forty years' period for their stay, showing that they conceived this time as parallel to the Desert Sojourn of the Hebrews." Thus the Jewish recital of history becomes in this sect more literally mimetic than in Judaism generally. But at the same time it is clear that they conceived this mimesis as the outward and visible sign of something essentially spiritual and ethical: they intended "to repeat the experience of their forefathers . . . while overcoming the trials through which that generation had failed to come successfully." So that the self-understanding at Qumran was essentially typological, an "applied typology" whose fulfilment was ethical, or at least involved ethics, and of which the sect's external conformity to the "accidents" of historical circumstances was merely a sign. They claimed that their ethical imitation of the "way of the Lord" would fulfil Israel's call, show them to be the true Israel—"the righteous remnant," indeed— and serve to atone for the sins of the nation at large.

That the same kind of principle has been at work in the Gospels, and, in particular, in these stories of the temptation of Jesus, need not surprise us therefore. There are the same overtly repetitive configurations of place (a wilderness) and period (forty days for forty years). There is the same awareness that these things themselves are symbolic of less "accidental" matters, the repeating of Israel's experience and the perfecting of Israel's response to the call of God, on the one hand, and the temptations of Satan, on the other. And there is the same sense that this obedience makes the obedient figure the true Israel, whose "remnant" is now concentrated in one individual, who may atone by his work for the sins of the people.

The attributing to Jesus of a personal repetition of historic events is therefore not in itself unique. Nor, indeed, is the idea of this repetition, the perfecting of the nation's response to temptation by a man or sect on behalf of the nation, unique either. What is unique is Jesus' perfect fulfilment of this aim, the achievement of perfect response to the moral demand on the people which the original Exodus-complex implied and had ever since symbolized. In the Qumran literature, the note of actual, present, fulfilment is absent. The Covenanters were impressed with the call but they knew that for all their attempts to respond they were sinful. But the Gospels present Jesus as himself perfectly obedient. He goes through the same temptation as Israel—as the answers, drawn from Deuteronomy 6–8, in Matthew and Luke, are probably intended to suggest—but he, unlike all others, truly perfects man's or Israel's response to them and so treads the "way" which the Old Testament, the Covenanters, and all "until John" only "prophesied" (Luke 16:16; cf. parallel in Matt. 11:12 f.).

Therefore if, as is asserted by J. M. Robinson, the fact that Mark 1:2–3 "offers a prophecy, and verse 15 speaks of the time having been fulfilled" means that we are "to look in the intervening narrative (vv. 4–13) for an event of fulfilment," then we can locate this event in the "initial victory over Satan" in the forty days' fast which Mark records and which Matthew, at least, interprets as the perfection of Israel's elected existence in the sole person of Jesus. In him the wilderness-people has at last stopped its "murmurings." It is because of this event that the evangelists can say that the time shift has happened and that history is now in process of being fulfilled; and, conversely, it is because they now see in Jesus the fulfilment of Israel's existence that they explain so much of his mission in terms drawn from Israel's history.

But before we elaborate this by examining further examples of the Jesus-Israel typology we should take stock of some of the inferences which may already justly be drawn. First, the idea of God's action which is essential to all proper typology. God's action in this case is his call to Israel which provokes a decision and therefore implies a temptation. It is as old as the wilderness journey and yet, because God is steadfast, always contemporaneous. Here it is made specific: Jesus, like the Israel of Moses, is led *by the Spirit* into the wilderness (Matt. 4:1; Exod. 13:18).

But biblical history includes not only the actions of God but the actions and reactions of man. If the initiative is always God's and God consistently takes it, the decision is always man's, who reacts toward or away from God's implicit call. Within any occurrence which brings man face to face with divine self-revelation—within God's act or its proclamation— his reaction (in either form of it) still implies repetition; man repeats his forefathers' rejection or repeats their surrender to God. Therefore my second point is that if typology really exists as an expression for the relation between acts of God, it must also involve a relation between acts of man in response to the old and new acts of God. So, in Jesus' response to a call like Israel's he repeats Israel's commitment, and perfects it.

Thirdly, we should note that it is the repetition of this response, the victory over Satan, the refusal to be tempted from his "way," that makes the temptation narrative typological. The repetitiveness of the setting here, like the symbolic configuration of numbers at other points in the Gospels, may or may not be "historical" but in either case points to the real, and really historical, parallel between the actions which they help to interpret—between, on the one hand, the actions of Jesus, which they "surround," and, on the other, the actions of Israelite history, which once they surrounded and henceforth (at least in Israel) recall.

Finally, we should, I think, notice how the concept of "history" with which we have worked makes sense in a special way of the idea of history's fulfilment. For places and times and people cannot in themselves be fulfilled by other places, times, people; but an emphasis on "actions" and "responses" already leads to a region of thought where the idea of "fulfilment" repeatedly shows itself relevant. For free, responsible actions have a purpose: purposes point to fulfilment and can be fulfilled. "Response" and "reaction," in turn, besides being "actions" themselves, also suggest something else, an obedience to some prompting, the fulfilling of a demand. Clearly, "demand," "prompting," "purpose," will often belong together on the side of the agent who takes the initiative in this dialectic; the fulfilment of the demand and the prompting in that case also involve the fulfilment of the purpose behind the demand and prompting. And in this case, so long as there is only imperfect response, the purpose, prompting, and demand are together only imperfectly fulfilled. We have only to see these points in terms of historical existence and they show their significance in relation to the Bible.

For according to the Old Testament it is the purpose of God that a new kind of historical existence should come into being. God "prompts" or promotes this existence by historical action on Israel. He demands (and the Law gives expression to this demand) that Israel should live this existence, that each Israelite should surrender himself to what God has prompted, should ratify the history in the response, should "fulfil" it. For, in the confession of faith, all Israel's history, in the last resort all human history, and even the Creation, has gone into the making of Israel's and the Israelites' opportunity for new existence. *Tua res agitur!*

But the other side of the same historical condition and conditionality exists in empirical fact so long as Israel's response is only imperfect. God's act and demand and purpose are only imperfectly fulfilled, "subfulfilled" within the Old Testament and within Israel's history before Christ. This, at all events, is the case as it is seen by Christian belief. But also, so long as the demand upon Israel exists and so long as the promoting activity of God is not broken off or undone, Israel's present existence in subfulfilment still points to a time which God's act and word promise, a time of future, perfect fulfilment, in which her existence in election will be (wholly) existent in empirical fact. At that time, the law, the promoting and prompting of Israel by God, and God's purpose revealed by past action, will together come to fulfilment along with the prophecies in which this existence is promised. Behind the typology of the New Testament lies the claim (not the

of Jesus remains, as the cry of the cross clearly indicates, "My God, my God, why hast thou forsaken me?" (Mark 15:34). Moreover, even though Jesus' intentions and actions are superseded by those of God, Jesus retains his own identity to the very end. He is not merged with God so that no distinction remains between God and Jesus. Nor do we mean to say that Jesus' intentions and actions become subordinate to those of God or that they lose their personal force. Indeed, the very opposite is true. Despite the decrease of initiative in Jesus, his intentions and actions, as well as his identity, retain their personal quality and weight. It is he who commends his Spirit into the hands of God and gives up the ghost, as Luke's Gospel climactically indicates (Luke 23:46). On the cross the intention and action of Jesus are fully superseded by God's, and what emerges is a motif of supplantation and yet identification. This motif is unlike a simple subordination of Jesus to God, for in such a case Jesus' intentions and actions, and hence identity, would bear no weight of their own. Instead, we see in the story a crucified human savior, who is obedient to God's intention and to his action.

This motif of supplantation and yet identification is one of the main themes of the liturgical hymn found in Philippians 2:6–11. In this passage, Jesus, though in the form of God, humbled himself, took upon himself the form of a servant, and was made in the likeness of men. "He humbled himself and became obedient unto death, even death on a cross." By virtue of this action God bestowed on him the name that identifies him above every name, Jesus Christ the Lord. Thus Paul, following an earlier tradition, depicts God's supplantation of Jesus' initiative in passion and death in terms of Jesus' obedience, in virtue of which he made God's intention and action his own, consenting to the divine initiative that willed his death.

But nowhere is the complexity of this pattern set forth more fully than in the Fourth Gospel. John stresses the dominance of the Father's will over that of the Son (5:19, 30; 6:37–40; 12:49–50; 14:28). He speaks of the Father's initiative over the Son in sending him (7:16, 28; 8:42; 13:16) and says that the Father alone has power to testify effectively to the Son. This claim of the Father's priority, however, is presented in such a way that the Son and the Father are nevertheless one (10:30). Hence both are glorified together in the Son's glorification (13:31–32; 17:1, 4–5). And though he who believes in the Son believes not in him but in the Father (12:44), nonetheless to believe in God is to believe in the Son (14:1); and to see the Son is to see the Father (12:45; 14:9).

Now, we should, for the sake of accuracy, say that in John's Gospel the balance between the dominance of the Father over the Son, on the one hand, and their unity, on the other, is delicate. These is, we may note, a tendency in the earlier part of the account (though we dare not push it too far) to underline the Father's dominance, in which it is the Father's witness to the Son that makes the latter's testimony true. The other aspect, their unity, tends to come to the fore gradually after its first outright mention in chapter 10:30. It gathers strength after the enunciation of the Son's hour of glorification (13:32) and rises to a climax in the great prayer in chapter 17 for the unity of the believers through the unity of Father and Son (especially vv. 21–26).

The theme we are talking about, supplantation or supersession in unity or identity rather than subordination, though articulated in greatest detail in the Fourth Gospel, is deeply embedded in the events of the story as told by the synoptic writers. In a sense their increasing stress on the rising curve or dominance of God's activity over that of Jesus reaches its apex, not in the account of Jesus' death, but in that of his resurrection. In fact, it is by virtue of this theme that one may and even must speak of a literary unity between the accounts of Jesus' death and those of his resurrection. That is to say, the authors' increasing stress on the dominance of God's activity over that of Jesus, starting with Gethsemane and Jesus' arrest, reaches its climax, not in the account of Jesus' death, but in that of his resurrection. It is here—even more than in the crucifixion—that God and God alone is active. Up to this point his efficacy had come increasingly to the fore in the steadily decreasing scope and activity of Jesus and the increasing tempo of the authorities' acts. Now, as the story comes to a climax, the stress is on God's increasingly direct and exclusive activity. But it is so in a peculiar fashion. For the hand of God, though obviously dominant and alone efficacious and directly present in the raising of Jesus, remains completely veiled at this point in the story.

The unanimous testimony of the earliest Christian commentaries on the events, such as Peter's sermons in the Acts, insists that it was indeed *God* who raised him from the dead, and that is, of course, the logic of both the situation and the story. As for the situation, could a person who is said to have raised himself really be said to have died? The logic of the story is similar. It presents us with a rising tide in which the will of God supersedes increasingly that of Jesus, moving by means of the "historical forces" that take charge. At the very crest of this tide we should expect God's will to supersede even that of the "historical forces" hitherto at work. And so it does, in its own manner, in the raising of Jesus. No other agency can possibly play any significant initiatory or even instrumental role here. Hence the earliest Christian preaching insists over and over again that "*God* raised him on the third day and made him manifest" (Acts 10:40; cf. 2:32, 3:15; 4:10) and that "we testify of *God* that he raised Christ" (1 Cor. 15:15).

But when we turn to the actual accounts of the resurrection, the hand of God is scarcely in evidence at this point in the story. In fact, the word "God" is hardly mentioned at all here. To some extent, this is due to the fact that the actual raising is nowhere described in the Gospels, and hence there is no direct appeal in the story to the agent of the act. Nonetheless, it is surprising that the absolute and direct initiative of God, reaching its climax at this point and stressed in the early preaching of the church, is completely unmentioned in the narrative itself. It is *Jesus*, and Jesus alone, who appears just at this point, when God's supplantation of him is complete. To summarize what we have said in a somewhat exaggerated form: In his passion and death the initiative of Jesus disappears more and more into that of God; but in the resurrection, where the initiative of God is finally and decisively climaxed and he alone is and can be active, the sole identity to mark the presence of that activity is Jesus. God remains hidden, and even reference to him is almost altogether lacking. Jesus of Nazareth, he and none other, marks the presence of the action of God.

In the narrative of the Gospels and the preaching commentary on it, Jesus is thus not simply in need of redemption but is, in fact, redeemed (Acts 2:24–32, 36; 13:35–37). The resurrection is the vindication in act of his own intention and God's. Moreover, in the unity and transition between his need for redemption and his being in fact redeemed, Jesus' identity is focused, and the complex relation and distinction between his identity and that of God is manifested. We have to add immediately, however, that there is no simple and direct coherence of the identity of the crucified and risen Jesus by means of one rhythmic or cyclical movement. The Gospels' accounts tell us quite clearly that the abiding identity of Jesus in the crucifixion and resurrection is held together by the unitary identity of him who is the same person whether crucified or resurrected.

The point is that we misunderstand the narrative if we regard the risen Lord as a phantom of the crucified Jesus or, conversely, if we regard the crucified Jesus as the earthly shadow or perpetual death stage of an eternally rising savior figure. Each of these stages has its own indelible uniqueness unexpunged, even though both are held together in the transition by which we move from one to the other. We may put the same point quite simply and in almost banal fashion: It was the crucified Jesus who was raised from the dead. The identity of Jesus who preached and died and that of the risen Lord are one and the same. As a result, the crucifixion remains indelibly a part of his identity, an event or act that is an intrinsic part of him. Thus, though the New Testament claims that Christ is genuinely present to believers as the *risen* Lord, its testimony is that it is the *crucified* Jesus who rose and is present. We can, we are told, no longer regard Christ, now risen, "from a human point of view" (2 Cor. 4:16); nevertheless, the one who is now present is no "spirit" (Luke 24:36–43), but the one bearing the wounds of his mortal body (John 20:27–29). He is none other than Jesus of Nazareth (cf. Acts 9:5; 22:8; 26:15). Thus Paul's experience on the Damascus road is clearly set forth in the Acts as an occasion for the self-manifestation of the risen Lord as totally identical with Jesus of Nazareth. The "I am" of the self-identifying remark, "I am Jesus," in that account has an almost Johannine force.

DID JESUS ENACT HIS OWN RESURRECTION?

In itself what we have just said may not appear to be a very startling claim, but let us say the same thing in a different way by proceeding from a parallel that has already appeared several times. We have said that Jesus' obedience to God and his steadfast intention to enact the good of men on their behalf hold together those personal qualities that would otherwise appear as unrelieved and abstract paradoxes. It is Jesus who holds power and powerlessness together, not they him, both in their simultaneity and in the transition from one to the other. It is likewise he whose intention is vindicated. He is, both in their simultaneity and in transition from one to the other, the Savior in need of redemption and the Savior in fact redeemed and redeeming. But this is really a very hard thing to comprehend, for it amounts to saying that he holds together his own identity in the transition from death to resurrection. Now, we have already suggested that Jesus' identity was what he enacted it to be in the crucial events leading from Gethsemane to his death. He was what he did. Are we then implying that he enacted his resurrection also? If not, how are we to understand the relation of God's and Jesus' intention and action in the structure of the New Testament narrative?

Whatever our answer to this difficult question is, we must stand by our affirmation that the unity and continuity of the narrative's structure is such—especially in Luke's account—that to leave out the climax furnished by the story of the resurrection (and even that of the ascension) would mean doing irreparable violence to the literary unity and integrity of the whole account. It would violate the story at its integrating climax. It would violate the story also to take this climax to be the "meaning" integrating the previous "events." Instead, we must insist that the story, as a connected sequence of events (with patterns of meaning embedded in it), comes to a climax in the story of the events of the resurrection and the ascension. Hence, the difficult question is inescapable: Since Jesus enacted his identity in what he did and underwent, and since his identity is the same—that of Jesus of Nazareth—in crucifixion and resurrection, does the story suggest that he raised himself from the dead?

To deal with this question we must stress again the fourth pattern in the Gospel story, that of an irreducibly complex pattern of interrelation between God's action and that of Jesus. We have already described it as one of supplantation by identification rather than subordination. The interesting fact about this pattern with regard to our present question is that, although God and God alone is the agent of the resurrection, it is not God but Jesus who appears.

THE RESURRECTION AS MANIFESTATION OF GOD'S HIDDEN ACTION

We spoke [elsewhere] of two types of identity description, intention-action and self-manifestation description. In the resurrection accounts, the two descriptions become intermingled. There, where God enacts his intention most directly (though veiledly), it becomes most clearly evident *who* Jesus is. Contrariwise, when Jesus' own intention-action sequence reaches its climax, in his passion and death, the question of his subject identity—who he is—is left most severely in doubt. The upshot of this subtle and puzzling issue is that the Gospel narrative presents us with neither a simple unification nor a simple distinction between Jesus and God, either in terms of intention-action or of self-manifestation identification. The pattern of their interrelation remains irreducibly complex.

To a degree, a pattern of unification prevails, in which Jesus is set forth in his resurrection as the manifestation of the action of God. This is in itself an odd way of speaking, for ordinarily the correlate of "action" is not "manifestation," but "enactment in public occurrence." "Manifestation," in turn, is the correlate of "presence" or "subject" rather than "enactment." Yet there is little doubt that exegesis of the Gospel story will indicate that in the resurrection Jesus is set forth as the presence or manifestation of God's hidden action. In this respect, then, God's deed in raising Jesus is actually a deed in which the identity of Jesus is *manifested*, rather than being the achievement of a historical *occurrence*.

Yet this particular emphasis meets a firm limit because the logic of the story and of the situation as well as the claim of the sermons in Acts all suggest that the resurrection of Jesus as an *enacted event*, and not merely as the *manifestation* of his *identity*, is the climax of the Gospel narrative. In this respect there is a clear distinction between God and Jesus, and there is an identification of Jesus through an intention-action sequence and not merely by means of self-manifestation.

More than this we cannot say in response to the strange but inevitable question, posed by reading the Synoptic accounts, Did Jesus raise himself? Obviously, he did not. And yet the complex pattern of unity in differentiation between God and him was not broken in the transition from crucifixion to resurrection. On the contrary, it reached its climactic fulfillment in the resurrection. We cannot simply say that the narrative pattern points us to the conclusion that where God is active, Jesus is not, and vice versa, or that where Jesus' identity is manifest, God's is not. Yet certain themes of this sort do appear in the story. Whatever further comment we may make on the identification of Jesus in relation to God, it is unlikely that we shall get beyond the pattern of unity in differentiation and increasing identification by supplantation.

The nature of the narrative therefore imposes a limit on theological comment. It is not likely that we shall be able to get beyond the descriptive accounts presented to us in the Gospels concerning the resurrection and the relation of God's and Jesus' actions. And if we do go beyond them in explanatory endeavors, we are clearly on our own and in speculative territory, just as we have suggested that we are in speculative realms when we look beyond the narrative for the writers' and Jesus' own inner intentions. In that instance, our speculation would be historical; in the present, metaphysical. But it is never easy and usually not desirable to transform a literary description, such as a narrative sequence, into an *explanatory* scheme using abstract concepts and categories. What is perfectly fitting in a narrative may be banal or absurd in an explanatory scheme drawn from our general experience of occurrences in the world. The task of transforming a narrative into such a scheme may be hardest of all in the case of the Gospels.

It is doubtless true that, since the narrative involves truth claims concerning facts and salvation as well as some lifelike and also some stylized religious elements, its eventual transformation into *conceptual* schemes was not only inevitable but even welcome. Descriptive schemes about such things as resurrection of the spiritual body were bound to come in its wake—and so, in the long run, were dogmas about the relation of the Father to the Son. However, necessary as such *descriptive* schemes may be, they cannot provide *explanatory* theories for the narrative's claims and for the various patterns of meaning inherent in it, and inherent in it in such a manner that meaning cannot be detached from the narrative form

A Struggle with Legion: A Literary Analysis of Mark 5:1–20

Jean Starobinski

They came to the other side of the sea, to the country of the Gerasenes. [2]And when he had come out of the boat, there met him out of the tombs a man with an unclean spirit, [3]who lived among the tombs; and no one could bind him any more, even with a chain; [4]for he had often been bound with fetters and chains, but the chains he wrenched apart, and the fetters he broke in pieces; and no one had the strength to subdue him. [5]Night and day among the tombs and on the mountains he was always crying out, and bruising himself with stones. [6]And when he saw Jesus from afar, he ran and worshiped him; [7]and crying out with a loud voice, he said, "What have you to do with me, Jesus, Son of the Most High God? I adjure you by God, do not torment me." [8]For he had said to him, "Come out of the man, you unclean spirit!" [9]And Jesus asked him, "What is your name?" He replied, "My name is Legion; for we are many." [10]And he begged him eagerly not to send them out of the country. [11]Now a great heard of swine was feeding there on the hillside; [12]and they begged him, "Send us to the swine, let us enter them." [13]So he gave them leave. And the unclean spirits came out, and entered the swine; and the herd, numbering about two thousand, rushed down the steep bank into the sea, and were drowned in the sea.

From *New Literary History* 4, no. 2 (Winter 1973). © 1973 by *New Literary History*, University of Virginia.

¹⁴The herdsmen fled, and told it in the city and in the country. And people came to see what it was that had happened. ¹⁵And they came to Jesus, and saw the demoniac sitting there, clothed and in his right mind, the man who had had the legion; and they were afraid. ¹⁶And those who had seen it told what had happened to the demoniac and to the swine. ¹⁷And they began to beg Jesus to depart from their neighborhood. ¹⁸And as he was getting into the boat, the man who had been possessed with demons begged him that he might be with him. ¹⁹But he refused, and said to him, "Go home to your friends, and tell them how much the Lord has done for you, and how he has had mercy on you." ²⁰And he went away and began to proclaim in the Decapolis how much Jesus had done for him; and all men marveled.

The attempt at a purely literary reading of an evangelical text has, without doubt, something of the nature of a wager: this reading is joined to all the preceding exegesis, of which it is ignorant or feigns to be ignorant. Because it is the reading of neither a believer nor even a theologian of another confession, it will seem inadequate by its very exteriority. This exteriority is not counterbalanced by the fact that it is encased within the interior of the text by an effort made to seize the whole meaning of it. For the one who applies himself to this kind of exercise, it is a test: will he be able to discern as many of the significative facts as the exegetical tradition has been able to see? This late comer knows quite well that his interpretation will be immediately compared with all those that have preceded his. He is then on his guard; he knows that he must be prudent and, conjointly, must take command of the resources of his ingenuity in order to prove the legitimacy of his methods. It will be difficult for him to adopt the attitude of the unbiased reader, whatever his desire to make a clean sweep, and to consider the sacred text as any other text: an abstraction cannot be made from the place of this text among the texts which mark out the centuries, from its historic function, and, consequently, from the present reasons (that is to say, historic) which we have for being interested in it. It is because of the procedure adopted and because of a cognizance that certain dimensions will remain elusive that one reduces the fragment in question to the sole register of its discourse, that is, to its structure alone. Certainly one will not go to the point of simulating ignorance of the Old or New Testament context.

What one sets aside is not the pages which precede and follow; it is the balance of the documents exterior to the text; it is all which, for the historian, contributes to situating the text in its time, by relation to events which do not figure in the narrative itself but which the scholarly memory has recovered along other routes. One may go ahead and accept without suspicion the canonical revision of the text without even asking if all the parts are indeed from the same hand and if there is room to discern any states anterior to the redaction which is offered to us. Briefly, in place of situating the passage within the context of historic time, we will strive to decipher the internal temporality which proceeds from its own statement. This amounts to studying the text in its "synchrony"—that is to say, in the quasi-simultaneity—of its parts, while giving, nevertheless, the most lively attention to its sequential organization: separating the text from the time of the historian, divorcing it from its immediate and remote conditions. The text is not immobile; rather it suggests a sense of duration which constitutes the very "thread" of which the docile reading makes an experiment. On these premises the analysis will renounce conjecturing how the text was composed, how it came to be written: the analysis takes the text just as it is given to reading. Such an exegesis concerns itself with all the elements as homogeneous givens, without claiming to distinguish what would be only "redactional" and what could be "original"; it will not vie with the historians in the search for a hypothetical narrative composed by the first narrators, glimpsed behind the enrichments of the distortions owing to the commentaries of the first community or to the literary processes of the evangelist. Structural analysis, instead of decomposing the traditional lesson, strives on the contrary to read the lesson wholly, and since it is, in this instance, a matter of a canonical lesson, we will pay closer attention to the form under which the text has been received and interpreted through the ages. This respect for the text takes into account the fact that in the course of generations it has been regarded as inspired in all its parts. It is under this form that it has operated. We are to know indeed that the most diverse alterations, be they arbitrary or accidental, do not abolish all meaning, but often offer another plausible meaning to interpretation: this contingency of the canonical text can cast doubt on its genesis and on its redaction, but not on the fact that it has been conserved and transmitted under the aspect in which we read it today. The accidents, the distortions, the corruptions and corrections can have taken place, and we do not ignore the fact that the most deformed text is still capable of speaking to us, of eliciting the ingenuity of the commentary, which bequeaths its unforeseen riches and assigns precise motives to it, where perhaps a copyist's blunder intrudes. The "risk" of any immanent analysis resides assuredly in its "too great" receptivity, in its consenting ductility, in its manner of adjustment to all that one submits to it. But nothing confines this type of analysis to the statement of harmonies and agreements: if it proves to be sufficiently alert, the analysis will point out also the disequilibriums, the eventual contradictions, the clashes between opposed processes, if it happens to encounter some of these. It may finally be that in a study which has begun by accepting all the givens which are proposed to it, it will be possible to decipher some inequalities, some disparities, some incoherences, from which philology will be able to profit for its own purposes of rectifying or setting aside doubtful elements. This is to say that a "critical" evaluation of the textual givens is not excluded a priori by internal analysis. But it is not in this direction that I intend to orient myself: it will suffice for me to address to the text a certain number of questions which await a response from it alone.

I. Who Speaks?

To what author (or speaker) does the text refer? There is no first person author at all in the beginning or in the last lines of the Gospel of Mark. There is nothing outside of the title which causes the name of Mark to appear. The text, then, is not suspended in the thought, in the will, in the memory, in the uncertainties of an individual. The "narrator" is entirely obliterated so as to protect his work from all that would render it relative to him or dependent on his particular point of view. This obliteration occurs not through modesty but in order to confer on his narrative the authority of knowledge without shadow. We meet here the very type of the pure narrative, whose radically narrative function excludes every expressive reference to the author. There is room only for the designation of a "referent" (the life and passion of Jesus) to which the destiny of all men is attached. From this comes the juxtaposition in this text of the simple narrative system which characterizes the *chronicle* and—in the preamble (1:1–3) as in the words cited (by John, by Christ)—of the *kerygmatic* attitude in which an advent and a decisive fulfillment are proclaimed. Not only does the evangelical text, like all mythical texts, unfold a narrative without explicit lacunae, where all the acts and words of the "hero" are faithfully reported in their entire purport, but it serves to fill the space of waiting and hope created by the text of the Old Testament and the prophets: it works for the filling up of the gaps in an antecedent text. In this way the textual citation of a word already written ("as it is written") and the verbatim citation of the word pronounced by Jesus ("he says:") come to stamp the text with an authority which can only reflect upon the narration (chronicle) which connects and introduces them. The discernible plan of the evangelist is to show that the suture has occurred between what has been announced and what is henceforth fulfilled: the suture is still more distinct when the citation of the Old Testament is found present in the very words which the evangelist puts in the mouth of Jesus. (Thus it goes from the first appeals of Christ: Mark 1:15, which takes up again Isaiah 56:1.) The question Who speaks? does not find then a single answer. The narrative, from which the *person* of the narrator is absent, introduces attributed speeches whose origin is strongly marked; there are then two levels to distinguish: that of the *pure* narration, exercising a presentative function, stating events and situation; and that of the reported words, which issue either from the Holy Book or from the person of Christ (and from those who approach him). The effacement of the narrator as subject then works in favor of putting Christ in evidence as the one who uses the *first person*: the evangelist speaks only to make another speak, without even attributing to himself the role of witness.

Nevertheless, he does attribute to himself complete knowledge of the identity of each of the personages (men or demons) who intervene in his narrative. He *knows* that Christ is the Son of God, and he can then distinguish those who have seen the truth from those who have not recognized it: this division renders possible a judgment regarding those who believe and those who do not allow themselves to be persuaded. The *certain* narration establishes the possibility of a line of cleavage and a separation which divides the contemporaries of Christ into two groups. But this line of demarcation is prolonged virtually until the moment of reading: for the one who takes cognizance of the evangelist's text, and who gives it his full adhesion as hearer or reader, the refusal to believe in Christ can only be the consequence of a blindness or a hardening. Through its judicatory form the text gives birth to a reading in which the judgment on the real identity of the personages immediately invites faith. Let us say, more distinctly, that the assent which accompanies every docile reading is here imperceptibly changed into an act of belief which, going *beyond that which is written*, is borne toward *the one of whom it is written*. The text is structured in such a way that the reader (or hearer) of the Gospel is made a disciple of Christ, ipso facto, by the interposed narrative.

II. To Whom Is It Spoken?

The text does not mention any explicit audience. It is not made final in a determined way. (It is by having recourse to some scattered clues that one can conjecture that the Gospel of Mark is "primitively" addressed to a pagan proto-Christian community.) But the absence of a determined audience has the effect of universalizing the recipient. The narrative unequivocally calls for a reading-recognition on the part of all people in every time. Christ, speaking to his questioners, in the circumstances defined by the narrative, reaches the reader not only in the measure that his words are sufficiently general to surpass the circumstances which provoked them, but also in the measure that the circumstances are suitable for assuming a symbolic function such that the readers might apply them to themselves.

III. Does the Text Contain the Clue to Its Own Status?

Present criticism, in the literary domain, is sensitive to details which, at the interior of a text, constitute the clue to, or symbol of, the function vested in the whole work, of the genesis or finality of the work.

We find in Mark 5:19–20 the order of Jesus given to the healed Gerasene: "Tell them." The man obeys: "[He] began to proclaim in the Decapolis how much Jesus had done for him." The man's reaction— his proclaiming—ensues from the miraculous moment of a healing; it is the result of an express order of the Master, who preferred that the man, restored to health, withdraw from him, in a distant mission, rather than accept him in the crowd of those who, at his side, accompany and listen to him. If the text of Mark is the act of announcing, of proclaiming, it carries, in this episode, a possible history—a figured symbol—of its own origin. It must be pointed out that this is one of the elements in the text which have attracted the suspicion of the historians: they see there a redactional addition, intended to justify by the very will of Christ, the mission, the apostolate, in non-Jewish territory. But that does not matter: it is under the "redactional" form that we read the Gospel of Mark, and it is particularly striking that the redactor believed it necessary to introduce here a "figure" of his own activity. (Certainly, in his effacement, the redactor is not present himself, and he does not relate the circumstances which led him to the faith: we cannot know if he himself was cured of a demon, whether by Christ or one of the apostles. But the expulsion of the demon, the deliverance, is in itself an act sufficiently rich in symbolic implications to be applied to every conversion, to every "new birth.")

IV. The Spatial Structure

Our text is particularly rich in spatial implications. Not only do we see a whole topography defined there, but this is revealed to us in terms of an action inscribed in it. We feel it is not a matter of a simple decoration; the very meaning of the action is in part tied to the space which it indwells. In other words, the action would not make sense if one removed the spatial determination from it: the action is inseparable from its movement.

"They came to the other side of the sea, to the country of the Gerasenes"—Kai ēlthon eis to peran tēs thalassēs eis tēn chōran tōn Gerasēnōn. The Greek text, by repeating the preposition *eis* (to), makes us attentive to a double specification of place. It is, first of all, the other shore of the sea (a purely topographic indication), and it is, moreover, the country of the Gerasenes (an ethno-religious indication). This abundance of information is not fortuitous: it is weighty with meaning.

Jesus passes into foreign territory, into the Decapolis (the country of Gerasa). Here are found herds of pigs, which one did not encounter on Jewish soil. Having crossed the confessional boundaries of the country, he will intervene in order to "save" a man, in order to make his witness, in the midst of a people who do not observe the law and have probably never observed it. One understands that metonymically the country of the Gerasenes might appear as the prototype of all the pagan territories, of all the Gentile countries where the Christian *mission* will spread. In that strain, the liberated demoniac becomes the prefigurement of the apostles, who constitute the models of every evangelistic enterprise.

But "the other side of the sea" is a "beyond" whose determination is not limited solely to the nature of the cults practiced in a foreign land. There is added immediately the whole series of features which confer on this place a wild and dangerous aspect: the tombs, the mountains. The Galilean shore was left at nightfall; the storm has arisen. And the first living being whom Jesus meets is a terrifying creature. One confronts here a series of cumulative traits which forbid us to consider Jesus' voyage as a simple passage from west to east. The crossing takes on a new qualitative nuance: it is the confrontation with a diabolical world; it is the equivalent of a descent into hell, of a *katabasis*. Through a metaphorical reading the other shore becomes the homologue of another diabolical world, and the voyage of Christ symbolizes a crossing of the universe to its darkest depths.

If the geographico-religious opposition (Jewish territory–pagan territory) offers the substratum of an ecclesiological allegory, the very image of the crossing to a wild nocturnal land peopled with demons allows itself to be read in an ontologico-theological sense: anagogically, the miracle worked by Jesus in these sinister places is a figure of universal salvation. The other shore is that which faces one from the outside, from the other side; it is the other, the inverse, not only in its quality of place opposite but also in its quality of opposing power. The shore beyond is an antishore; the day beyond is an antiday; the tombs, abode of the dead, are an antilife; the demons are rebels. The *crossing* of the "frontier" is the central event, qualified to function as a decisive sign both in the ecclesiological allegory and in the ontological reading. Christ goes toward the other: adversary, unbeliever, suffering man. One sees that the two meanings of the crossing—to vanquish (the demon), to convince (men)—do not exclude each other. Indeed, the one rather confirms the other, for the two significations are not competitive: one can hold them to be consecutive, the liberating action constituting the point of departure for the "evangelistic" mission entrusted to the healed demoniac.

For our part, we will see some of the text's active functions as centering in words or groups of words apparently without importance, but which receive a great weight of meaning from their repetition and from the words with which they enter into relations: the preposition *eis* (to, into) which appears at first in order to indicate the movement of Christ ("to the other side") reappears in order to indicate the movement enjoined upon the healed demoniac ("go home to your friends"). The positive dynamic is strongly inscribed in the prepositional structure thus repeated: it is a matter each time of a *movement toward*, having a sense of confrontation, and of the propagation of salvation (of the truth in salvation, of the narration regarding the healing). One will notice immediately that the same preposition reappears as though to figure the counterpart of the liberating movement, when the spirits enter *into* the pigs and when the pigs rush *into* the sea. These actions can then be interpreted as the movement of that which flees and recoils before the presence of Jesus. The fall of the pigs comes to cut a vertical dimension (the fall from high to low) which contrasts with the horizontal of Christ. We learned that the possessed lived "among the tombs and on the mountains"; thus from the mountains to the depths of the lake the course of the demonic powers literally crosses that of Jesus.

The global sketching of the action in space is closely tied to the movement of the persons, and this would not describe the movement appropriately if one omitted to point out that its origin is found, most generally, in the word of Jesus, who announces it and, as it were, engenders it. The crossing is made known in 4:35: "On that day, when evening had come, he said to them, 'let us go across to the other side.' " The movement is then *spoken* before it is *accomplished*. It is the same with the mission of the liberated Gerasene. In 5:19 Jesus *says* to him: "Go home to your friends." Then in full obedience the Gerasene complied: "He went away" (5:20). There is room to ask if this antecedence of speaking to accomplished action is not a characteristic structure of our text (and beyond Mark, of all evangelical and prophetic literature). The event is prespoken, whether in the remote past, by the Scriptures, or in the shorter span, by the word of Jesus, master and prophet, whose power is attested by the confirmation which each event brings to that which he has uttered.

We have previously underlined the role of citation in Mark (and it is a trait which is repeated in all the Synoptics): verses of the Hebrew Bible and words of Christ are designated with the same level of exactness—which, in order to convert a Jewish hearer, should have the effect of confirming the same authority, the same degree of certitude, on the word of Christ as on the text of the prophets or the psalmist. Now, how is one to define this process if not as a way of attributing to the scriptural text the predictive function in the prediction-fulfillment relationship? In a first sense Christ, his teaching, his sacrifice have been predicted: they fulfill what has been promised and announced, in the last instance by John. In a second sense the word and action of Christ are themselves predictions; they announce (as the prophets do) events to come, of which some are realized in the short run and others are meant to be realized in a future less precisely determined. The evangelical text offers us then a redoubling, or even a tripling, of the predictive function:

A. According to what is written: Hebrew Bible ⎫ Person of
   According to what John has announced: John   ⎭ Christ
B. According to what He has said: Words of Christ ⎫ Immediate or
                                         ⎪ distant events
                                         ⎬ predicted by
                                         ⎭ Christ

In our text Jesus does not announce or enjoin anything that is not realized immediately. But it is not the same everywhere: Jesus also announces some things whose fulfillment remains to come. How can it be otherwise? If Jesus' coming had fulfilled to the point of saturation the promise and expectations inscribed in the prophetic books, peace would have reigned visibly on earth. As this is obviously not the case, the evangelist can declare the former prediction fulfilled only by opening up—in the heavenly dimension—a new promise, that is to say, by having new prophecies uttered by the one who comes to fulfill all the previous ones.

If the relation of the antecedence of the word to the prominent event (punishing, healing, betraying, etc.) seems habitual to us, then every event of any importance, if it is not "explained" by an antecedent word, is fated to be perceived as an anomaly and to cause perplexity to commentators. Thus it is in our text with the plunge of the pigs into the sea. All that is attributable to the word of Jesus is the injunction of expulsion: "Come out of the man, you unclean spirit." Jesus does, moreover, accede to the entreaty of the spirits to enter into the herd of swine: "So he gave them leave." The plunge into the sea is neither predicted nor ordered, from which the reader receives the impression of the absence of every causal connection. That the destruction of the herd might have been willed by Jesus can only be the object of a hazardous inference and is thus subject to discussion. It is more profitable in fact to hold to the statement that it is here a matter of an event not preceded by the word, and from this fact, of an event which we can attach neither to an intention nor to an injunction. The event then becomes even more available for a purely symbolic interpretation: the plunge of the pigs into the sea is a figure of the fall of the rebellious spirits into the abyss.

V. THE PERSONS

It does not escape the simplest examination that Jesus is related to a multitude of persons and that his relationships are in a constant state of change.

It is necessary to enlarge the field of our examination and to note that the departure from the Galilean shore (4:36) as well as the return to this shore (5:21) are underscored by the presence of the crowd: in order to be able to embark with Jesus, the disciples have dismissed the crowd; and as soon as Jesus is back, a crowd is gathered around him. We discover a kind of symmetry. With regard to the Galilean crowd, Jesus has been successively present, then absent, then back again. In his relation to the crowd, Jesus accomplishes the movement of distancing himself and of reappearing, which will be his movement once more, in his relation to the apostles—at the time of the crucifixion, the entombment, and the resurrection.

In the passage which runs from 4:35 to 5:21, it is worthwhile, moreover, calling attention to the number of personages who surround Christ or confront him. Jesus is at first in the midst of the crowd (4:35); then he is found with his disciples in a boat surrounded by several other boats (4:36). Later on, the narrative mentions only the single boat of Jesus and the disciples; in 5:1 the text makes mention of a collective arrival: "They arrived." But Jesus alone is named when the departure from the boat is mentioned: "when he had come out of the boat" (5:2). And it is a single man who comes to an encounter with him from the depth of the tombs. We have witnessed, then, in the course of the text, a progressive singling out of Jesus both because he effectively distances himself from the others (the crowd, the other boats) and because the narrator has decided to speak only of him without taking account any longer of the presence of the disciples who have escorted him up to this point. The disciples will be evoked a posteriori as those who had seen what had occurred. Everything happens as if the narrator had wished to give the greatest possible emphasis and dramatic intensity to the confrontation of Jesus and the demoniac, by conferring on the scene all the characteristics of a single combat.

But beginning at this point we are going to witness a pluralization in which those who face or surround Jesus are going to be progressively multiplied. Already the man who comes to meet Jesus is said to be captive to an unclean spirit. The adversary is then double. He will become legion, will swarm in a herd of two thousand pigs. One will see arriving successively the swineherds and the people of the city and the country, that is to say, a whole Gerasene crowd which, instead of keeping Jesus, beseech him to leave their territory. It is then that Jesus again finds the crowd which he had left on the western shore of the "sea."

Jesus, permanent hero of the evangelical narrative, is the immutable representative of the singular. The disciples form a group with him only in a precarious and unstable way: a variation in their faith can separate them from him at any time. Jesus, then, is not found connected with others in a relation of faithful belonging together. He cannot be the equal of anyone: his role as master, healer, liberator commits him to a perpetually asymmetrical relation characterized most often by the singular-plural opposition. Jesus teaches *the crowd,* then distances himself from it in the company of his disciples; but, as if to maintain the singular-plural opposition, the crossing is marked by the storm and by the reprimand of Jesus to the disciples (4:40). The dramatic face-to-face encounter of Jesus and the demoniac at first sight gives to *the other* the appearance of a unique individual; (the other becomes legion) but, on the one hand, we will discover that it is not for long and, on the other hand, it must be added that the absence of the *numerical* indication of the singular-plural opposition is compensated for by the accentuation of the *qualitative* indication of the Good-Evil opposition, or Son of God/Demon. The structure of opposition remains undamaged. And one will add that the healing of the Gerasene, his conversion to a disciple of Jesus, his evangelistic mission have the effect of conferring upon him the privilege and danger of singularity, with reference to the teaching which henceforth will be his among all the inhabitants of the Decapolis. The Gerasene (sanctified and purified by his encounter with Jesus) will face alone all his pagan fellow-countrymen as Jesus faces alone all those whom he teaches and heals. One can say, then, that Jesus addresses himself to plurality, to the crowd, but that his efficacious intervention is eminently singularizing, individualizing, for the one whom his intervention reaches. And it is not wrong, it seems, to add that evil is always on the side of plurality: whether it be a matter of illnesses, demonic hostility, or unbelief, the adverse element is always plural. One will recall here Kierkegaard's formula: "The crowd is untruth." But it must be observed that Jesus hardly ever ceases to encounter men and to manifest thereby his power through healings and *singular* conversions.

A minute examination of the pericope Mark 5:1–20 shows us admirably, almost as if it were the effect of an intrinsic necessity, the process of the impure spirit's pluralization. In 5:2 there appears a man with an unclean spirit. We meet here a singular term with a double referent (man, spirit). When the man, in 5:7, prostrates himself before Jesus and addresses the word to him and beseeches him, it is still in the singular that he speaks: "What have you to do with me, Jesus, Son of the Most High God? I adjure you by God, do not torment me." Let us add that we have here a very ambiguous singular, by means of which the man as well as the demon can express himself. The supplication is addressed to Christ, a clearly designated recipient, but the speaker does not exactly make himself known. The first person singular, which admits only a single subject, is manifestly too narrow: from this results a mixed blurring of the two essences (man and demon) based on the one "I" ("me"). In response Jesus addresses the unclean spirit in the singular, as if he were ignoring provisionally his plural nature: "Come out [plural form of verb] of the man, you unclean spirit" (5:8). And it is while still attributing to him a singular nature that Jesus asks him his name: "What is your name?" The demon himself had instantly recognized Christ and had hailed him as Son of the Most High God: it has often been observed in reading the Gospels that the demonic powers— because they are "spiritual"—are instantly able to recognize the identity of Jesus, their mortal enemy. Would Jesus be less clairvoyant facing the demon? Or must we admit that the question posed to the demon is not a true interrogation, but is already the beginning of the combat with the adversary. To compel him to surrender his name is to render him vulnerable by means of the foothold which it offers henceforth to exorcism. Now the name which the demon surrenders to Jesus is a singular collective: "My name *is* Legion." This name (although singular) is a multiple term: it is the key to the pluralization. Forced to confession by the irresistible pressure of Jesus, the demon utters his identity. The term "legion" is rich in implications and connotations which one can easily discern: it multifariously designates the military, the hostile troop, the occupying army, the Roman invader, and perhaps those who will crucify Christ. From now on the plural can be displayed: "For we are many." The same voice which said "my name" says immediately "we are": it has become a collective voice, and we are surprised *here* by a paradoxical effect of anacoluthon. A syntactical cleavage disengages a new subject (plural) from the preceding subject (singular). However, in 5:10, we discover once more an oscillation between singular and plural: "And he begged him eagerly not to send them out of the country." The following sentence (5:11) causes a collective singular to appear again (the herd), but its complement (of pigs) immediately determines its plurality. With the resumption of the verb "to beg" the subject is definitively plural, although the identity of the demons remains implied: "And they begged him, saying . . ."

(5:12). Finally the subject is manifested fully in its quality of nominal plural and verbal plural: "And the unclean spirits came out." The expulsion of the powers of evil occurs, one sees, according to certain stages in which the exterior objectification is accentuated: the surrendered name, the progressive pluralization are already an outcome forced from the person of the possessed man. The entry into the body of the animals and the plunge into the sea will only bring about the completion of the movement of exteriorization, giving the deliverance its quasi-hyperbolic expression. The departure from the man (*exerchesthai*) is completed by the entry (*eiserchesthai*) into another host. The prefixes (*ex, eis*) are weighted with a strong and rudimentary value, marking the crossing of a boundary toward the outside (*ex*) or toward the inside (*eis*). At the end of the process of deliverance, a triple crossing will have occurred: out of the man, into the body of the pigs, *into the sea.*

Readers have wanted to see in this text the echo or residue of a folktale about the devil deceived. What has undoubtedly stimulated such an interpretation is the fact that the story related here ends (provisionally) in a perfect *return to order*, after beginning with an original situation of disturbance. Through a supernatural intervention a man has been thrown out of his community; the demons have ventured out of their proper place, which is the abyss. The hero intervenes, and his action (here his efficacious presence, for there is no real struggle) has the effect of putting everything back in its true place: the man among his own, the demons in the depths. The story is then completed by the rout of the wicked rebel and by the reestablishment of what had been disturbed. Everything is ended, or seems to be, so as to satisfy the need for redress which animates such a great number of folk narratives. Jesus appears as a hero assured of victory, right away he is *the strongest.* The interest is not placed on the combat itself but on the circumstances of the defeat of an adversary who, for everyone other than Jesus, has been an object of terror, on account of his strength and his wickedness. One notices all the signs of sovereignty on the side of Jesus; the imperative statement, the question (both in direct style), the permission to enter into the body of the animals (in indirect style) are expressed with extreme economy. The utterances of the demon are prolix: there one discerns the desperate maneuver of an adversary at bay, who multiplies supplications and proliferates in vain. Jesus, the hero, subdues the one whom no one had the strength to subdue (5:4). Moreover, the redress (as in numerous narratives) comprises an increase of success, a supplementary gain: the healed man is not only returned to his own but becomes a follower of Jesus, he joins the one who has healed him, just as liberated captives, in the popular tale, perform an act of allegiance to the liberating hero.

And to the pluralization of the powers expelled there corresponds an inverse process—of individuation—for the liberated man. The ambiguous subject who utters—"What have you to do with me?" (5:7)—is broken open in order to give issue to the unequivocal plurality of the unclean spirits and to permit conjointly the freeing of a human subject returned to his singular identity. The expulsive catharsis separates decisively the invaders and the being previously occupied by them. The aggression turned against himself in 5:5 (in the act of bruising himself with stones) is transferred to the pigs who cast themselves into the sea. The self-destructive violence has been displaced. This violence, essentially brutal and brutalizing, rediscovers its appropriate habitat in the body of the unclean animals.

VI. Jesus Recognized, Jesus Rejected

From the time of Jesus' arrival we have viewed the possessed man and his address conferring on Jesus his full identity: "Jesus, Son of the Most High God." On the other hand, the people of Gerasa, despite the story of the witnesses and the testimony of their own eyes, beg Jesus to leave the country (5:17). They have not recognized him.

This contrast between recognition and nonrecognition prompts the posing of the question: Who recognizes Jesus? Those who have the power of vision recognize him: from the beginning of Mark it is successively John the Baptist, and the demoniac in the synagogue at Capernaum (1:24), then the "unclean spirits" who greet him as Son of God (3:11). Jesus, moreover, seems desirous of not being recognized: "But he strictly ordered them not to make him known" (3:12). Mark then attributes to Jesus the will to teach and to heal while not allowing himself to be openly recognized. The disciples themselves remain in doubt about his spiritual identity. As for his relatives (3:21) or his fellow townsmen from Nazareth (6:1–6), they are able to see only his earthly identity: they fail entirely to recognize the divine aspect of his person and his teaching.

Let us pose a new question: How is the opposition to the central figure of Jesus manifested? Who plays the role of his opponent? The pericope of the Gerasene demoniac permits us to reply; at first it is the demon, and then it is the Gerasene crowd who ask Jesus to leave their territory (5:17). The nonrecognition then takes the place, in the human world, of the clairvoyant opposition of the demonic powers in the spiritual world. (The failure to recognize, the nonrecognition, could then appear as the human figure of the hostility of the demon.)

But let us examine more closely the way in which Jesus confronts the two oppositions. In the pericope of the Gerasene demoniac Jesus confronts the demons; he exorcises them, expels them, and departs from this encounter with the enemy as a victor. The adversary has yielded before him and has hastened to his fitting ruin. But this event, which the evangelist relates with full knowledge of the facts, is not recognized as a beneficent miracle by the Gerasenes: they become afraid (and one may conjecture that their terror, in the eyes of the evangelist, is of the same nature as that of the witnesses who suppose, in Mark 3:22, that Jesus is himself *possessed by Bulzebul,* and that *it is by the prince of the demons that he casts out the demons*). Now, while Jesus had engaged in combat with the demonic adversary and defeated all opposition from that quarter, he does not resist the human adversary. He leaves the territory, delegating to the liberated demoniac alone the task of facing henceforth the unbelief of his fellow countrymen. Thus after Jesus' victory over a first opponent (a victory which signals and attests his divine mission), one sees a continuing residue of opposition at another point, a hostility which is not allowed to be reduced and which Jesus, moreover, does not undertake to overcome.

It is not a matter here, it seems to me, of a position limited to the pericope which we are analyzing. Let us consider what immediately precedes (4:35–41). There we see the storm arise during the crossing of the sea: the violence of nature puts the boat in danger. Awakened from his sleep by the anxious disciples, Jesus instantly calms the waves. From the far reaches of a state of weakness and apparent absence, Jesus exercises through his word an irresistible power over the elements, which obey him immediately. There is here a vanquished opposition: a great calm follows upon the storm. The disciples lack faith; they know Jesus only by the title "teacher." The miracle worked by Jesus arouses in them, not full recognition, but a great fear, for which the evangelist has recourse to the same verb as that used for the blind fear of the Gerasenes. Thus the identity of Jesus remains for the disciples a question without answer: "And they said to one another, 'Who then is this, that even the wind and sea obey him.' " These words, which I indeed believe should be given a sense more interrogative than exclamatory, allow us to understand that the disciples are still incapable of perceiving the "real" nature of the power exercised by Jesus. The narrator himself claims this knowledge and can thus contrast the *vanquished opposition* (this time, in the world of natural elements) and the *residue of opposition* which continues in human consciousness. Such then is the paradox of a narrative in which one sees the hero triumphant in relation to natural (wind, storm, illness) or supernatural (the demon) opponents, while he allows human opposition to reappear and persist. But the paradox is a matter of a *narrative* which would dry up if new "tests" did not reappear progressively. The residue of opposition, the resurgence of hostility, provokes the continuation of the narrative. And as the lot of all men is at stake, the continuation of the narrative is the equivalent of the continuation of the story, and indeed of history.

In fact, the resorption of all opposition to Jesus would be the absolute calm, the disappearance of all evil powers, the end of time, the submission and reestablishment of all things in the divine order—in a word, the *visible* fulfillment of all the ancient prophecies. The task of the evangelist in general is to announce that the Messiah has come and to show how, throughout his earthly ministry, the victory accomplished was still only preliminary, *prefiguring* other victories made necessary by an opposition reappearing without cease. Thus there are conjointly enough tests of Jesus' divinity and enough obstacles which compel the postponement of the total pacification of the world to project the latter into a dimension of future hope. The opposition never completely disappears. Rather, it is reconstituted along other lines; it retreats, one would say, according to the system of "elastic defense," taking other forms—as many successive forms as are necessary to occupy the duration and to sustain the waiting for the radical disappearance of evil.

The pericope whose analysis we have just sketched has made us present at a movement of victorious expansion: expansion in objective space, on the soil of a foreign country; expansion of the divine word which makes the powers of evil retreat and which liberates their captive. The calamity of the pigs can then appear, we have said, as the figure anticipating the fall of the rebel angels. But it is only the figure and promise, for the movement of expansion is stopped by the unbelief of the Gerasenes. The movement is inverted; Jesus, chased away, takes the road back: he lets the "converted" demoniac face, perilously, the opposition.

Is this structure not found again at other levels? If we envisage in its entirety the whole earthly ministry of Jesus, it is constituted as the expansive movement of a truth which heals bodies and wins souls: the residue of human hostility informs the trial and passion of Jesus. Jesus no more protects himself from that than he protected himself from the inhospitality of the Gerasenes.

In its turn Jesus' resurrection occurs as a victory over the most cruel opposition: Jesus is stronger than death. But the residue opposition reappears immediately in the human world. Jesus sends the apostles into the whole world, but he foresees the resistance and the damnation of those who will not believe: and he said to them, "Go into all the world and preach the gospel to the whole creation. He who believes and is baptized will be saved; but he who does not believe will be condemned" (Mark 16:15–16).

An eschatology which foresees the eternal separation of the elect and the damned thus projects into eternity a residue of hostility— destined for punishment, not restored and resorbed into the unity. But could an eschatology promising, for its part, the reconciliation of the entire creation eliminate the concept of the opponent? I believe not. In order to announce a *final* time when all things (including evil itself and wicked men) will return to God, it is necessary to stress all the more that which, in the *present moment*, creates an obstacle, hinders a return, foments the persistence of evil. There are without doubt theologies filled with the most ardent hope of final joy which have the greatest need for a concept which enables men to exercise patience by explaining to them why they are not yet in the promised blessedness. (It is the same thing with certain forms of political faith which are only secular theologies.) In order to give form to its residue of hostility, it will be necessary to invent the anti-Christ. One will come in some way to confer on every form of opposition (unbelief, disobedience, violence, etc.) the demonic shape which it takes in the text we are reading. And, in the course of time, with regard to the demonized opponent, the combat will be entrusted to exorcists, if the temptation to conquer by the sword is not to prevail.

VII. THE PARABOLIC INTERPRETATION

The sampling of a pericope is not an innocent act. It is always permissible, certainly, to have an analysis bear upon a narrative fragment, confined within sharp limits, and tending to reclose upon itself as soon as one examines it in isolation. But a step of this kind tends to cause the global text to be read as if it were composed of a series of episodes, in the first place independent, then sewn end to end. The episode (here the pericope) then appears as the constitutive unit whose structure and "function," once put in evidence, will be repeated identically, or in an homologous way, in all the other narrative segments. Now we are not able to put any stopping places at the two boundaries of the text studied. It is necessary to have the limits of the next move at every moment. This is what we have already done in considering the pericope of the calmed storm. But let us ascend again the way of our text and consider Mark 4:1–34 and what is said to us there about teaching in parables. Let us reread in particular these words of Jesus (where the memory of Isaiah 6:9–10 is evident): "And when he was alone, those who were about him with the twelve asked him concerning the parables. And he said to them, 'To you has been given the secret of the kingdom of God, but for those outside everything is in parables; so that they may indeed see but not perceive, and may indeed hear but not understand; lest they should turn again, and be forgiven' " (Mark 4:10–12).

The hearers are separated into two groups by Jesus: "you," and "those who are outside." We discern immediately the antinomic inside-outside opposition. And when Jesus declares: "He who has ears to hear, let him hear" (Mark 4:9), we notice an opposition quite as radical: *he who has ears as opposed to he who does not have ears.* Teaching in parables seems to assume here a limiting and defensive aspect: it is closed to those who do not have ears, and by the same stroke it closes access to salvation. Far from being motivated by the pedagogical concern of giving an imaged approach to the truth, recourse to parable deliberately limits the number of the elect: it keeps out those who do not have understanding. One could suppose further that in establishing this separation the parabolic form of teaching works to preserve a factor of opposition, a nonreception of the message. All the greater will be the merit of those who will have acceded to the full meaning or who will have had the privilege of hearing Jesus interpret the parable. Thus in the parable of the "Sower of the Seed" one must understand the "word" itself. In the case of the nature of the earth into which the seed falls, it is necessary to guess that the parable designates the interior dispositions of the hearers. The birds which pick up the seed are an image of Satan, etc.

If one keeps to the parable itself in its double version, everything happens as if the nonreception of the message were imputable to a cause exterior to the message itself; the fault devolves upon the soil

character divides the audience in two, according as the "second" meaning has or has not been perceived. Now here the possibility of opposition arises: for the opponent is above all the one who is caught in the earthly literality and wants to see in Jesus only a man like other men. In that case the disguise of Jesus prevails. The eschatological meaning has indeed to exist for the evangelist, the end of time is postponed as long as opposition persists. This very opposition, nevertheless, when it takes the form of the crucifixion, plays an essential role in the economy of salvation. It is necessary that there be men who do not understand. The trope must remain obscure to certain people. The descent of the word into the parabolic form is then the way of its manifestation—of the only possible manifestation of the truth here below—and it is, conjointly, the way in which the will of the Son of God secretly stirs up the opposition which, while bringing about the fulfillment of the scriptural prophecies (Mark 14:49), imposes an indefinite delay upon the final victory. As long as the parable lasts, with its double semantic level, an earthly kingdom persists to present obstacles to the kingdom of God. But the opposition is overthrown in promise; thus the waiting of the prophets is prolonged: the prophecies are *fulfilled*, but the kingdom of God is still *to come*. Everything is already *said*, but everything is not yet *understood*. The story continues and, with it, the parabolic narrative and the necessity to interpret it.

VIII. HOW TO INTERPRET POSSESSION

Engaged as we were in the analysis of a narrative, we have not discussed the question of demonic possession, a question concerning which one expects the mediation of doctors, historians, etc. Why were there so many demons in the Palestine of Jesus? Is it necessary to invoke external influences—especially Mesopotamian? Must we accept the suggestions of those who see in the loss of political autonomy one of the causes for the transfer of interest to sick individuals and their healing—to psychic health and the salvation of the soul? These are problems which require a positive investigation, in which there is no question of being engaged here. We are content to examine to the best of our ability the description—the narrative—of a case of demonic possession and its miraculous cure.

There is one point, however, which merits discussion. The conception most currently accepted among historians of science is that cases of demonic possession offer us a good example of the way in which a natural phenomenon receives a cultural interpretation. Demoniacs were, it is said, individuals presenting spectacular symptoms—such as we meet today in epileptics or schizophrenics. Mental disorder, given in fact, receives a signification through the interpretative tools which the language of an epoch (or a civilization) has at its disposal. The object to be interpreted is the violence, the agitation, the cries: the interpretative tool in the first century is the concept of demonic possession. The interpretative operation, in our text, is accomplished *without remainder*. Everything seems to be explained in this way. The development of a language of medical theory will constitute a new system of conceptual tools and consequently permit the possibility of a reinterpretation. It is rare that a specialized language should not claim the right to extend itself to all that it can include and desire to prove its applicability to domains hitherto covered by another type of discourse. For example, in the history of medicine, when a physiology of the circulation of the "winds" in different parts of the organism was elaborated, Hippocrates had at his disposal a natural explicative system which supplanted the concept of the "sacred malady." When the discourse on the equilibrium and disequilibrium of the four humors was systematized, one could assign to melancholy a good part of the disorders of the spirit, and the rationalist doctor then had at his disposal an instrument which permitted him to challenge the concept of demonic possession. The latter interpretation appeared henceforth as an *unwarranted* interpretation of a series of phenomena which could more simply be reduced to the interference of an excess of black bile in cerebral operations, and so forth.

But let us be aware that the notions of nature, natural causality, distribution of "winds," excess of humor, etc., are themselves interpretative instruments, elaborated by different historically dated languages (or discourses), subject to change and revision, even if, since Hippocrates, they have in common the presupposition of the "non-supernatural" character of the worst anomalies of behavior. Every interpretation which believes itself to be adequate claims for itself conformity to "the nature of things." It prefers not to conceive of itself as an interpretation but as a statement of what in truth occurs, while reserving, with a pejorative nuance, the term "interpretation" for all the preceding readings of the same given, readings which seem to it tainted by illusion, encumbered with imaginary projections, deformed by the prejudices of the interpreter. Surely, as it is a matter of setting forth the "facts," their causality, their signification, modern science is more conscious of having given rise to them by an active intervention; it does not flatter itself with the thought of having interpreted them without remainder. It advances an "explanation" only after having tried all the counterproofs which the experimental procedures at its disposal permit: it admits that its discourse in its turn might be supplanted by a better endowed discourse. It is ready, then, to conceive that which it affirms as an interpretation among other interpretations.

Therefore, let us state that what we designated a moment ago as the natural given (schizophrenia, epilepsy, *athétose*) has nothing of the fundamentally natural. Perhaps, rather than using terms borrowed from the discourse of present-day medicine, we should have remained solely in the "phenomenology" of the acts mentioned by the evangelist: solitude, wandering, crying out, violence, self-inflicted wounds.

However acceptable the idea might seem that a series of facts, of givens, would *precede*, in virtue of being the first stratum, the interpretation subsequently given to them (here, the wild solitude giving place to the explanation by means of possession), one cannot help suspecting that the opposite is also admissible. One can indeed maintain that the "view of the world," in Jesus' epoch, and still more in the epoch of the evangelist, stressed to such an extent the opposition between the rule of God and the rule of the demonic that it elicited from those who appealed to it a set of *signs*. Therefore, it is no longer the morbid symptoms which are primary but the "cultural" concept of demons, which becomes explicit through the agitation, screams, etc. The disturbed behavior, the screams, the violence are then the means through which the individual interprets and actualizes the presence of the demon, of which he has been previously informed by theological discourse, as well as by everyday conversation. We know such to have often been the case in the epidemics of demon possession which raged in the sixteenth and seventeenth centuries. It is the same with hysteria, the definition and clinical picture of which, circulated in written or oral form, played an often determining role in the onset of the most exemplary cases of that disease. One can then speak of the sociogenesis or the logogenesis of the symptom.

I do not think that one should exclude the first hypothesis, according to which the notion of demon possession functions as an interpretative tool, applied to an antecedent given. But it is necessary to see a circularity beginning here; the concept which may have been at first an interpretative tool becomes in its turn a given offered to living interpretation. Can one determine a starting point? Is there somewhere a truly primary and natural given? The more attention one pays, the more he sees the natural substratum recede; when man comes into the picture, one always finds nature "altered" by culture and language.

In the epigraph of *The Possessed*, Dostoevsky has placed Luke 8:26–39, which corresponds to the passage which we have analyzed here. Must we assert that the novel is a developed interpretation of this passage from the Gospel? Must we, on the contrary, consider that the evangelical text, elevated to the rank of interpretative tool, should permit us to interpret the narrative of the novel, to grasp its meaning? Here again interpretation reveals its circular aspect. The positions are exchanged: that which must be understood becomes that which permits understanding; that which permits interpretation becomes that which must be interpreted. Have we not stated something analogous with regard to parable? We underlined at that time what in the parabolic message was profoundly dependent on temporality. One must say the same thing of the circle of interpretation: it has room to develop only because at the same time that he is a speaking being, man is a historical being, destined for change but desirous of acceding to meaning.

The Women at the Tomb: A Structural Analysis Essay of a Gospel Text

Louis Marin

Our subject is limited. It consists of analyzing a short story which we have read in Matthew (28:1–8), Mark (16:1–8), and Luke (24:1–11) which reports the arrival of the women at the tomb of Jesus which they found empty. This analysis will be neither complete nor exhaustive. It will remain at what A. J. Greimas calls the superficial structures of the narrative, while throwing out some hypotheses for the elaboration of the codes implemented by the texts examined. Moreover, this study of the surface structures could only assume its full value beyond the arbitrary limits of the texts envisaged by the integration of the narrative in the global narrative of the Passion and Resurrection of Jesus which should also be submitted to an analysis of the same kind.

One of the working hypotheses which could be given for an analysis of this kind and which ought to be tested and verified would be the application of the functional and mythical actantial model which was worked out by A. J. Greimas from the works of Lévi-Strauss, Dumézil, and especially Propp. At first glance and in a general way, one can construct the following actantial model of this whole narrative:

From *The New Testament and Structuralism*, edited by Alfred M. Johnson. © 1976 by the Pickwick Press.

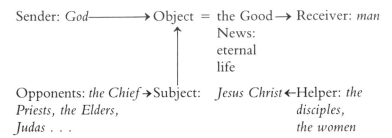

On the other hand, the functions of the global narrative could be developed according to the following schema:

I. Contract: mandate The Son of Man goes to be delivered
    acceptance   in order to be crucified.

II. Succession of three tests:
  1. qualifying   The anointing at Bethany
  2. principal   All the crucifixion sequences
  3. glorifying   Revelation of Jesus

This last test is characterized in the Gospel narrative by the multiplication of partial tests (the meeting of the women and the angel at the tomb, of Mary [who mistook him for the gardener], and Jesus, of the Emmaus pilgrims and Jesus, the recognition by the touch of Thomas, etc., and finally the recognition by the community of the disciples). However, one should note one remarkable trait in this redundancy of glorifying tests: only the recognition of the resurrected Jesus by the community is effective and genuine. *All the other recognitions made by individuals fail.*

Nevertheless, we will emphasize in order to take direct aim at the specificity of the texts considered, the process of displacement that *these* particular texts have undergone in the general model applied to the global text. In effect, the narrative of the women at the tomb can be characterized from this point of view in the following way:

1. As far as the general actantial model defined above is concerned, the women who belong to the *helper* actant in the global narrative, are found here in the *subject* position. The angel, on the other hand, possesses the helper status, but he is also a *mediator* between the sender, God, and the receiver, who is basically formed here by the disciples as a society or community. Therefore our narrative defines the general receiver, humanity, as a religious community.

The *opponent* actant is perfectly represented: (a) by the sealed and rolled stone which refers to the general actant which is defined in the global narrative as the priests and elders of the people (these are the ones who have positioned the stone in front of the tomb so as to prevent a possible fraud by the apostles intending to give support to the prophetic discourse of Jesus: "I will rise from the dead in three days"); and (b) by the soldiers.

As for the *object* actant, which is defined as the Good News announcing eternal life, the narrative makes us see a *displacement* of its content.

The intervention of the angel, who is an object of communication, and the message "that Jesus has risen" comes to be substituted for the object which at the beginning of the narrative, is the object of the "quest" of the women and the object of desire which is defined as the dead body of Jesus. We will return later to this most important point.

2. *As far as the functions are concerned,* our narrative is well organized as a "micro-test," which is defined at the beginning as an established state of a lack or an absence and at the end by a liquidation of the lack. However, this liquidation is not effective but only *virtual* since it only takes place in the verbal form of a message which is either not transmitted or not believed. In short, it is not completed by recognition (= negative micro-test), or if one prefers, considering the end of the global narrative, it is virtually positive.

ANALYSIS OF THE TEXT

We have arbitrarily chosen Matthew's narrative as the guideline for this analysis, and we will use the other parallel narratives as variants. This narrative is divided into four main parts:

1. The arrival of the women at the sepulchre
2. The arrival of the angel
3. The angel's discourse or the delivery of the message
4. The departure of the women and the transmission of the message

Part 1. The Arrival of the Women at the Sepulchre

This sequence includes three elements: (1) the spatial-temporal index; (2) the subject actant (or helper in the position of the subject): the women or the woman; (3) the object actant: the tomb.

(a) The spatial-temporal index gives us the beginning of an

especially interesting code. There are two temporal indexes in Matthew. There is the index of a *religious or liturgical ritual time*: "After the day of the Sabbath"; and there is an index of a *profane cosmic time*: "as the first day of the week began to dawn." The opposition of the religious and profane marks, therefore, the determination of the moment. This is an opposition which is also found in Mark but not in Luke. However, between Matthew and Mark, on the one hand, and Luke (and especially John) on the other, a new opposition takes form within the profane or cosmic time, i.e., that of light and darkness. On the one hand, there is "the dawn" and "as the sun was rising"; and, on the other hand, there is "very early" and "as it was still dark." Thus a double interplay of oppositions—light/darkness, profane/sacred—emphasizes the initial moment of the text. There is an opposition whose common characteristic is a beginning or a commencement. It is a question of a new sacred week (after the Sabbath), a new day, and a new profane week. Therefore the profane and the sacred coincide on the temporal plane, and in this sense they are respectively beginnings or commencements. But they are also opposed to one another in that the sacred week is characterized as *past*, and the profane week is characterized as *beginning*: "after the Sabbath"/"the first day of the week"/"the first moment of the day."

This new opposition is correlated with the light/darkness opposition. The last hour of darkness is the first hour of the day; the end of the last day of the Jewish holy week is the beginning of the first day of the "Christian" week. In other words, we have a stage of a *passage* through a *threshold*, that is to say, to a *reversal* of the old/new and Jewish/Christian times (cf. the threshold rites of passage), and to the creative, initiatory moment of a new cycle.

This spatial threshold (the opening of the entrance to the tomb) which constitutes the preoccupation of the women corresponds to this temporal threshold according to the triple dimension of profane/sacred, nocturnal/diurnal, and Judaic/Christian. A space is *closed*, i.e., the tomb by the stone. One must replace this closed space with an *open* space, i.e., the stone must be rolled away. Matthew presents a truly cosmic "production" of the opening of this space, i.e., an earthquake, which, by upsetting the natural world order (a closed cosmic space) has the effect of opening the tomb.

The emptiness of the space corresponds to the opening of the sacred space of the tomb. At the same time, the crossing of the threshold [i.e., door] of the tomb has revealed its emptiness. Therefore there is a twofold interplay of spatial oppositions: opening/closing, fullness/emptiness (of the space).

Finally on the plane of the global narrative, this spatial opening and this temporal passage refer to another beginning, to the overture (in the musical or dramatic sense of the word) of the third glorifying test. This is the overture of a new sequence of the narrative.

One will note that one can see the same phenomenon of overture which is like an echo (Matt. 27:51–53) at the time of the death of Christ (which marks the end of the principal test when the disqualification of the hero takes place): the Temple curtain (which closes the Holy of Holies) is torn in two. The rocks and the earth are split; other tombs are opened. Thus there is a double opening of holy, religious space (the Temple and the tombs) and cosmic space (the earth and the earthquake).

It is notable that this spatial overture, which is at the same time an initiation of a new temporal cycle, is connected to the resurrection which is also defined as an *exit* into an open space. The tomb is a holy closure like the Temple, time, and death. To rise from the dead is to leave the tomb; it is to open the sacred space to the dimensions of the cosmos; and it is to open death's door which may be conceived as closed.

(b) The subject actant: the women. Neither their proper names nor their number appear to be pertinent traits. There is a question here of a *"female" class.* No doubt, it would be interesting to examine thoroughly the status of this particular actant in the global narrative and especially to define precisely the feminine inflexion of the global "helper" actant and the nature of its relationship to the "hero" actant. We will return to this point in the functional analysis of this narrative, but let us note as a hypothesis that the women are a modality of the function of *desire* or the quest. More precisely, they appear in this particular narrative as the *initiators of the final test.* In the hierarchy of the receivers of the message, they are the first ones to receive the good news, but at the same time, they are the "weakest" intermediaries.

(c) The object actant is the tomb, but it is the tomb insofar as it contains the dead body, i.e., the tomb as symbolic of a corpse. This relationship clearly appears in Mark. It is implicitly present in Luke in the sequence which interests us, but it is explicit in sequence 3. The angel says: "I know that you seek Jesus Christ who was crucified." The object of the quest is Jesus Christ insofar as he is the one who was crucified. It is the death body which *fills* the tomb, hence the body puts a system of correlations into action:

(1) *Dead body* (= cadaver) which one can *touch* (unction)	(2) *Living body* as an object which one can *touch,* with which one can enter into contact, either directly or by the mediation of this container which is the clothing (cf. the miracles which have contact with the body, e.g. Mk. 5:25–34)
(3) *Living Body* as an object which one cannot touch (cf. the *Noli me tangere* [= "Do not touch me." John 20:17])	(4) *Living body* as an object which one can *touch* (cf. the skeptical Thomas)

Contact appears here as a taking possession of the living or dead body, but always as a phenomenon of passivity. The body is offered or offers itself as an *object* unlike the active contacts which are produced, for example, in the miraculous healings. Hence there is a system of oppositions here.

In this sense, the episode of Thomas, who is skeptical of Jesus' resurrection, is similar to and the opposite of the episode of Mary Magdalene in John's Gospel, just as the anointing at Bethany is similar to and the opposite of the arrival of the women at the tomb.

(d) The general function of sequence 1 is that of the desire or the quest of the object. The desire and the object of desire are put in the religious and ritual context of the Law.

See the Gospel of Peter 50–57:

> Now early in the morning of the (day) of the Lord, Mary Magdalene, a disciple of the Lord . . . , taking her friends with her, went to the tomb where he had been laid. And they were afraid that the Jews would see them and they said: "Ever since the day when he was crucified, we have not been able to weep and lament, let us now at least approach his tomb. But who will roll away the stone for us, which has

been placed against the entrance to the tomb, so that, being admitted, we can be near him and do what we must? For the stone was great and we are afraid that someone will see us."

The accent is put on the notion of ritual and religious duty: "to mourn," "to lament" / "to anoint the corpse," "to do what one ought to do."

It is important to define precisely the place and meaning of this ritual of unction or embalming of the cadaver in Judaism. But in any case, it is probable that this ritual was intended to preserve the cadaver. In this sense, this funeral ritual is a symbolic form of the accomplishment of the desire for the preservation of the corpse which mimes the possession of the body.

This is the reason for the interest in and the importance of the anointing at Bethany which constitutes a sequence opposed to sequence 1 of our narrative (Mark 14:3–9, Matt. 26:6–13, John 12:1–8). A woman qualified the body of Jesus to be a corpse by anointing it at Bethany. The women qualify the corpse to be a body by anointing it at the tomb. In the first case, the gesture of the woman at Bethany is a stage in the qualifying test of the hero. She qualifies it for the test of death or for this negative principal test which is the crucifixion. In the second case, the gestures of the women constitute a kind of symbolic qualification for the glorifying test, i.e., for the return and recognition of the hero as living beyond death. But this qualification is symbolic because the body of Christ has risen from the dead and will be recognized as a living body, while the anointing by the women at the tomb *was intended to preserve the body* as a dead body.

The whole meaning of the narrative will consist of the frustration of the immediate (but also symbolic) accomplishment of the desire. However, its accomplishment is delayed; it is mediate but real ("he has risen from the dead").

This analysis permits us to return to the status of the woman:

1. She has a relationship with death (the weeping, burial of the dead, their embalming). The desire is realized symbolically (but perfectly, that is to say, immediately) in death.

2. She has a relationship with the hero, but it is an individual and emotional relationship of possessive passivity: hence the anointing contact, the passive touching of the object.

This double relationship is opposed to: (1) the affirmation or recognition of the hero as alive, but with a "difference," in other words it is a postponed but truly realized desire; (2) the affirmation or recognition of the hero by the community of the disciples in a relationship which is no longer individual but communal.

This double opposition is an inflexion of two very deep semic categories: life/death; individual/society.

Part 2. The Arrival of the Angel

(a) *The index of the arrival of the angel.* We will not return to the earthquake which is the spatial index of the irruption of the sacred into nature and the opening of profane space. On the other hand, it is necessary to investigate thoroughly the second index of the arrival of the angel which is his clothing. The angel's clothing is characterized by its absence of color (white) and its brightness. It is resplendent and as dazzling as lightning. It would be interesting to investigate white clothing—which dazzles and blinds one and in some way annuls the real, carnal, solid presence of the angel, while affirming it at the same time. In any case, one can establish a relationship between the brilliant white clothing of the angel and the substitution of the presence of the angel for the missing body of Christ. This substitution is more remarkable in Mark and Luke than in Matthew. The women appear in order to see, touch, and anoint the corpse in order to preserve it. They find one angel or two angels in dazzling whiteness.

The angel, by its brilliant presence, annuls the dull presence of the corpse which was sought and desired. There is an annulment of the object of desire here. That is the reason for this hypothesis: the brilliant whiteness of his clothing is at the same time an index of the irruption of the sacred, but it is also an index of the absence of the real, human object of desire. At this point of the discourse, we could define the double opposition in this way: presence/absence and supernatural/ human (or sacred/natural) but with this characteristic: the sacred is negatively defined as the annulment or obliteration of the real object of desire.

(b) *The actants:* The angel is presented as a helper but equally as a designation of the sender actant. It is the angel of the Lord who descends and comes from heaven. The angel is a mediator in the position of a helper of the subject (the women) because he repudiates the opponents, which are the stone and the guards. He rolls the stone away and makes the guards tremble from fear or strikes them dead.

On the whole, the angel is an operator who opens the sacred space of the tomb which is closed and guarded by the stone and the soldiers.

Note 1: In a way, sequence 2 is parallel to sequence 1. The conjunction between sequence 1 and sequence 2 will take place in sequence 3. Sequence 1 is positive: the subject is in quest of the object which is the object of the desire. Sequence 2 is negative: the helper repudiates the opponent, but at the same time the helper erases the object of desire, the walk of the women to the tomb ends without the object.

Note 2: The narrative contains a blank or empty space which is, properly speaking, the resurrection sequence, i.e., the sequence of Christ's exit out of the tomb which the Gospel of Peter (35–44) restores. One can describe this blank space as an ellipsis in the linguistic manifestation which only gives us the consequences. The height of omission is reached in Mark and Luke where the angel does not roll back the stone but where the women find it rolled away or displaced (cf. Mark 16:4; Luke 24:2).

Moreover, this lack signifies to us that the subject of the statement is identical to the subject of the enunciation in the three Synoptics. In other words, the redactor or the narrator of the narrative described the scene as the women would have described or related it. There is, however, an infringement of that rule in Matthew where the arrival of the angel and the earthquake are described. Have we also read this description of the angel, less in its referential aspect than in its stereotypical, indicative aspect?

Part 3. The Discourse of the Angel

The discourse of the angel can be analyzed in three segments which are framed by two instructions which open and close the discourse. These instructions are the modalisators: first of attitude, "Do not be afraid," or even of the opening of the discourse; second of closing or the closure of the message: "Lo, I have told you!"

The three segments are defined as:
1. the recognition of the quest and the absence of its object,
2. the recalling of the message of Christ,
3. the deliverance of the angel's message which is to be transmitted.

1st segment: "I know that you seek Jesus Christ, who was crucified; he is not here." This is an affirmation which is accompanied by its counterproof: "See the place where he lay," which one can symbolically transcribe in the following way:

If q = quest, and p = presence, then we have q + p here.

2nd segment: "He has risen from the dead as he said." This is a discourse here in the second degree which is recalled from the discourse of Christ which announced his resurrection or = $\overline{\text{non } p}$.

3rd segment: repeats the discourse in the second degree, but it is not in the form of a quotation but is like an order or an imperative. The discourse in the second degree here becomes a message, properly speaking. It can be transcribed: $\overline{\text{non } p}$ + $\bar{q}$. "He has risen from the dead; he goes before you to Galilee; you will see him" = the quest is repudiated by its satisfaction.

If one agrees to transcribe the opening discourse as a, the opening of the discourse to the second degree as α, the opening of the message as α', and the indicator of closure as b, this sequence can be written:

$$a\,(\,q + \bar{p} + \alpha\,(\text{non }\bar{p})\,) + \alpha'\,(\text{non }\bar{p} + \bar{q})\,b$$

1st degree	2nd degree	Message
discourse	discourse	
(1)	(2)	

The advantage of this "symbolic" transcription is to make one see that the message is a negation of discourse (1) and a repetition developed from discourse (2).

One can draw some conclusions from this analysis. The first is of a general nature. One sees here—and the definition of this *actor* "angel" as a substitute annuler of the object of desire prepares one for it—the substitution of the message for the desired object. More precisely, the absence of the object of desire is filled by the presence of a message which: (1) affirms the absence of the object of desire *here* and *now* but gives this absence as a positive modality of this object; and (2) affirms the presence of the object as *already* and *elsewhere,* but in the form of a message to be transmitted (the message is *present*). That is the reason for the *substitute* equation: absence of the real object here and now = presence of the message whose referent is always present and already elsewhere. One could say in Hegelian language that one sees here in the passage (by the negativity) from the reality "*here, now*" of the object, to the discourse of the "*always—already—there*" and to the discourse of omnipresence or rather the transformation from desire of the object to communication of the message. The desire is like a mediator of communication.

The second conclusion concerns the content itself of the angel's discourse and especially the symbolic terms α and α' which are transcribed respectively as "he has said" (or according to the translations "as he had said") and "Tell" (or "Go, tell").

"I know that you seek Jesus who was crucified" is an assertion of the quest whose constative aspect is strongly marked by "I know that. . . ."

"He is not here, because he has risen as he said." "He has said" clearly states, in a kind of equivalency, a negation and an affirmation which are not on the same level and do not belong to the same act of discourse. "He is not here" is an empirical proof which flows, as a consequence, from the preceding proof of the quest: "you seek Jesus. . . . He is not here." (One will note a reinforcement of the proof in Mark: "Behold the place where he was laid.") On the other hand, the affirmation "he has risen," is the repetition in an indirect style of a word of Jesus said *long ago* or *previously*. But this repetition has the effect of making it contemporary with the enunciation of the proof "he is not here." At the same time, this simultaneity establishes an equivalence between the proof that he is not here and the affirmation pronounced *long ago* by Jesus "I will rise from the dead." In other words, the proof is a realization of a prophetic word and it is only that. The prophetic word, which is recalled and established in the form of a quotation by the angel, makes the body of the crucified one disappear, if one can say that. He *makes himself disappear now*, by having said long ago. . . .

"Go, tell his disciples, 'he has risen, he is in Galilee, you will see him.' " The third part of the angel's discourse modifies the internal perspectives anew. Benvéniste's definition of the performative is "a declarative jussive verb construed with a *dictum*." But this *dictum* (which is the prophetic word cited in the preceding segment) is also at this precise moment of the discourse a *factum*, a proof which it is only a question—but it is essential—of making known. Likewise, the angel's order does not rest on the presence of Jesus in Galilee, his resurrection, or his visibility, but on the proclamation, the disclosure of this presence and visibility. Perhaps this is a fundamental function of the prophetic word which transforms the *dictum* into a *factum* which gives the full consistence of a fact and an existing event to what is said. It is twice said in the angel's discourse that Jesus has risen from the dead. But the first time, in reference to Jesus' word, a *factum*—the absence of the dead body—is a *dictum*: "I tell you, I will rise from the dead." The second time, this *dictum* is a *factum* by the speech act of the angel, a proclamatory order: "Jesus has risen from the dead; he goes before you into Galilee; you will see him there."

Thus, on the one hand, a discourse in the second degree appears in the heart of part (3) of the narrative, which opens with the expression "the angel said." It belongs to the order of the narrative in general and is opened by an expression such as "Christ has said." And, on the other hand, there is a message which (insofar as it still belongs to the narrative in the form of a linguistic object) is substituted for the object of desire, but which displays, moreover, a nonnarrative dimension, since it is of a proclamatory type: "He has awakened from death; he is somewhere else and already present."

Third conclusion: the women seek Jesus Christ as a cadaver and a mute object. They find the angel who is a speaking messenger delivering a message. The angel by himself is, in a way, a message since he is substituted for the object of desire. But at the same time he delivers the message. The angel affirms the negation (if one can say that). He shows the absence of the object of desire to be a presence which is somewhere else and living, that is to say, a message (i.e., a linguistic object present here and now). There is the mark here of a passage to what one could call the universality of the message or the index of the substitution of the discourse *for the referent to be verified* and of a message as a *sign to be believed*, which does not designate the absence of the referent, but signifies, in the absence of a referent, the presence of the word.

Part 4. The Departure of the Women from the Tomb

One must distinguish two segments here: the departure of the women from the tomb and the transmission of the message to the community of disciples. These two segments are modalized in a complex way, on the one hand, by what one could call a dynamic spatial modalisator, i.e., the speed, "they ran, they departed quickly . . ."; on the other hand, by an effective or emotional modalisator which is twofold: the fear, indicative of the angel's message and more generally of the irruption of the sacred into the profane; and the joy, indicative of the content itself of the message.

On this point, one will note the disagreements (which are perhaps significant) between the text of Matthew (which is our guideline) and the texts of Mark and Luke which function as arbitrary variants in our reading. In effect, we note the disappearance of the notations of fear and joy in Luke and that of joy in Mark.

Moreover, one should note the variants of Mark and Luke, concerning the second segment of this part. The message in Mark is not transmitted: "They said nothing to anyone." The message in Luke is indeed transmitted materially and physically, but a fifth part is added to the four parts of the story which defines a failure of the denotative, cognitive, or referential function of the communication: "Their words seemed to be nonsense (to the apostles), and they did not believe them."

In a more general way, one can say that part 4 of the story is that of the transmission of a message by the women, but it is a message which is not or only partially received. From this point of view (and the dynamic and spatial point of view), part 4 is indeed the opposite of part 1. In the first part, the women come to the tomb, if not with haste, at least with eagerness (i.e., early at daybreak). In the fourth part, the women leave the tomb quickly, in haste. In the first, they come in order to anoint the dead body; in the fourth, they transmit (positively, negatively, or partially) the message which structurally signified—and one should weigh the "ideological" importance of this conclusion—that *the message has repudiated the dead body and the transmission has repudiated the unction.*

There could be an unction only if there is a dead body. Now the dead body is missing and in its place there is a message. Thus does the nontransmission of the message in Mark, which is itself physical, signify that the women in this "variant" are left with everything which the ritual of unction includes and which we have tried to define? In other words, the closing in relation to the dead body which is an individual relationship to the object of desire, while the transmission of the message reveals the substitution of the message for the object of desire and the substitution of the communal relationship for the individual relationship. One would then understand the disappearance in Mark (which is a "variant" of the nontransmission of the message) of the emotional modalisator of the sequence: the joy, which one finds, on the other hand, contradictorily combined with fear in Matthew.

In conclusion, from this partial and incomplete analysis of many of the planes, one could reconstruct this characteristic trait which is revealed from an implication, which is perhaps universal, concerning the Christian religious text and which the short story of the women at the tomb could illustrate: namely, that there is an apparent narrative in which another story is secretly told, that of the passage from a discursive figure focused on the natural human or supernatural event. It is a discourse *which says something* to another discursive figure. The former is not focused on the context as Roman Jakobson said, but on itself and its texture, on its elaboration, or even more precisely, on its own communication and its own transmission. This is the unusual stage in the narrative where the things, the referent, or the bodies fade away and are missing and where the *paroles* and the messages appear in their place like bodies and things, in short, where the words become things (cf. Michel Foucault, *The Order of Things*).

CRITICAL NOTE 1:
ON THE MODEL

The methodological questions, which we pose concerning the application of this semiotic model to the analysis of this text are twofold:

The first is that the constant utilization of this narrative structural model does not lead to a loss of some semantic "substance," which the specific character of the narratives examined equally lose, rendering the formation of the underlying codes in this particular narrative discourse all the more difficult. Now it is indeed *this* discourse which interests me, and not the general abstract model whose emergence will be selective and combinative.

Second, in possession of the model, we are not in danger (at the level of the methodological practice) of making the text (considered in its manifestation) undergo some distortions, simplifications, etc., so as to make it more manipulable on the formal plane. This is the technical problem of the preparation of the text which one encounters in the analyses of myths, narratives, or poems. But the procedures which one employs rests on the linguistic code common to the transmitter and receiver and essentially on the form of the expression. Can one give the same justifications when the modifications or alterations are based, or risk being based, on the substance of the content? Therefore, it would be fitting, in order to clarify these points, for a rigorous epistemological analysis to be undertaken on the subject of

the utilization of the notion of a model and on its metaphorical
function, etc.

CRITICAL NOTE 2: CONCERNING THE FUNERAL UNCTION

At the very least, this is the explicit meaning of the text: "If she
has poured this perfume on my body, it is in order to prepare me for
my burial that she has done it." The unction is indeed an anointing for
death which is practiced on a living and not on a dead body. Therefore
there is an inversion of the order of the actions: it is not at all: 1st to
die, 2d to anoint the dead; but: 1st to anoint the living person, 2d to
die. However, one knows that the unction is also the ritual act of
enthronement of the kings of Israel. Thus one reads in 1 Samuel 10
that at the time of the inaugural institution of kingship, Samuel took a
small flask of oil and poured it on Saul's head, then he embraced him
and said: "Has not Yahweh anointed you as the leader of His people
Israel?" This enthronement is also performed by the falling of the spirit
of Yahweh on the royal elect: "Then the spirit of Yahweh will fall on
you, you will go into a delirium . . . and you will be changed into
another man" (1 Sam. 10:6). Thus one can wonder if the anointing at
Bethany is not also an unperceived royal anointing (only its mortuary
function has been decoded by Jesus). It is an anointing which, unlike
the other anointing which precedes or anticipates the ritual moment of
realization, here follows it because the royal messianic entrance had
already taken place and the eschatological prophecy had already been
proclaimed. "Decoded" in this way by the most discerning decoders,
Mary's revelation conceals an excess of meaning which the story does
not reveal in its literality. It appears on the surface in the present case
because the interpretation belongs to the story. But the story contains
the signs of a growth of meaning. They are signs which call attention
to the syntagmatic order, since it is the ordinal position of the actions
on the axis of combinations which draws attention to this surplus of
meaning.

But one must add a note which raises a new problem. This is the
knowledge of another text, that of 1 Samuel, which shows (in Matthew's text which relates the anointing at Bethany) a correlation with
the messianic entrance. The problem of the closure of the text, that of
the relationship of the text and the context, and the limits of this
context are also indirectly articulated in this text which we are studying. This is because the knowledge of the ritual of anointing belongs to

the textual order, but it could also arise from decorated monuments, bas-reliefs, or paintings which would then enter, in some way or another, into the perhaps endless interplay of textual references.

CRITICAL NOTE 3: A DEFICIENCY IN THE REPRESENTATION

Moreover—and this is the main point here—the fact that the resurrection escaped representation, if it was representation which the narrative deploys in its manifestation, the fact of grasping the event in its negative results and not in its sudden appearance, permits me to transfer the whole weight of the narrative, its whole gravity—and thereby its significance—on the angel as the vector of the word. And of what word? That of the resurrection of Jesus. The narrative, by not showing the event, separates itself from the representation in order to impart to the word what the representation would have represented, the event in the world of the escape of Jesus from the tomb and from death. The Gospel texts make the resurrection of Jesus something that cannot be staged. They remove it from the fiction (of the fable) of the narrative in order to entrust it to the discourse. It is by refusing to relate it that this thing of the world, this fact which must be proof and truth of all the later preaching, which they make expressible in words, that is to say composes it in a fundamental statement of discourse. This is, in the text itself, the *reality* of the Good News. We will return to the analysis of the angel's *discourse*.

CRITICAL NOTE 4: THE BODY-WORD

One should thoroughly investigate and situate this permutation at diverse levels and points of discourse of the constative and performative modalities in a larger problematic. In any case, it is characteristic of this element of meaning which seems to be important to us: the double conversion of the referential quotation in a proclamatory message and from a fact of speech to a speech of fact. It is to this extent that the message in this text constitutes a linguistic ensemble which has the value of an injunction, an obligation, and a quasi-realization. It is a *fact* which appears in and by the *word*.

Furthermore, the angel's discourse indirectly gives a reading lesson in the interplay of the living word to the women. It teaches them to *read* the facts and events, like a text, where the spaces, absences, or blanks signify—forever—some fillings or presences, but it signifies them *elsewhere*: in Galilee, in the future—"You will *see* him; he *precedes* you." These are presences of which the entire "conclusion" of the Gospel is the quest and which will only be found in the form of a descent and proliferation of the word. Whatever teaching—the empty space—the impression or the trace—left by a dead body uncovers is nothing else than the inscription of the word, "I will rise from the dead."

Hoti's Business: Why Are Narratives Obscure?

Frank Kermode

> *He did not speak to them without a parable.*
> Mark 4:34

> *He settled Hoti's business.*
> BROWNING,
> "A Grammarian's Funeral"

If we want to think about narratives that mean more and other than they seem to say, and mean different things to different people, with a particularly sharp distinction drawn between those who are outside and those who are inside, we can hardly do better than consider the parables.

A parable is, first, a similitude. "With what can we compare the kingdom of God, or what parable shall we use for it?" (Mark 4:30): here the word for parable—*parabolē*—could as well be translated "comparison," and sometimes is. It means a placing of one thing beside another; in classical Greek it means "comparison" or "illustration" or "analogy." But in the Greek Bible it is equivalent to Hebrew *mashal*, which means "riddle" or "dark saying," but I gather it can extend its range to include "exemplary tale." Sometimes the Greek word is also used to translate *hidah*, meaning "riddle."

Riddle and parable may be much the same: "Put forth a riddle and speak a parable to the house of Israel," says Ezekiel, proposing the enigma or allegory of the eagle of divers colors and the spreading vine

From *The Genesis of Secrecy.* © 1979 by Frank Kermode. Harvard University Press, 1979.

(17:2f.). The saying of Jesus that nothing enters a man from outside can defile him is called by Mark a parable; it is not especially dark, but dark enough to call for explanation.

What is interesting about parables from the present point of view is first this range of senses, which seems to reflect pretty well all the possibilities of narrative at large. At one end of the scale there is a zero point, a strong saying, perhaps, with no narrative content to speak of; and at the other is the well-formed story which, as structuralist exegetes like to demonstrate, exhibits all the marks of narrativity. But there is another scale to consider. Parables are stories, insofar as they *are* stories, which are not to be taken at face value, and bear various indications to make this condition plain to the interpreter; so the other scale is a measure of their darkness. Some are apparently almost entirely transparent; some are obscure.

All require some interpretative action from the auditor; they call for completion; the parable-event isn't over until a satisfactory answer or explanation is given; the interpretation completes it. In this respect it is like a riddle, sometimes a very easy riddle, sometimes one of the comic kind that contain interpretative traps: for example, the riddle that asks how you fit five elephants into a Volkswagen, which can only be answered if you ignore the hint that it has to do with size; it has to do only with number. But it is more usually a tragic riddle, like that proposed by the Sphinx to Oedipus—if you can't answer it, you die, for that is the fate of the outsider who sees without perceiving and hears without understanding. Or we might try another comparison, and say that the interpretation of parable is like the interpretation of dreams, for the dream-text, when understood, disappears, is consumed by its interpretation, and ceases to have affective force (or would do so, if one were able to conceive of a completed dream-analysis).

But this notion, that interpretation completes parable, and there's an end, is much too crude. The parable of the Good Samaritan, to which I'll return, ends with a question: "Which of these three, do you think, proved neighbor to the man who fell among thieves?" There is only one possible answer: "the Samaritan." Or so it would appear to common sense; though common sense is not our business. The answer may leave an interpreter unsatisfied, because a narrative of some length, like the Good Samaritan, works hard to make the answer obvious and in so doing provides a lot of information which seems too important to be discarded, once the easy act of completion is performed.

When parable stretches out into short story commentators sometimes say that it has escaped from the genre altogether; so they call the Good Samaritan and the Prodigal Son "example stories." But that, in my view, is dodging. They are indeed parables, though as far from the pole of maxim or riddle as one can get; they are about to merge into long narratives, which may also retain some of the qualities of parable. Think, for instance, of *Party Going*. Of course between these extreme points—the maxim and the short story—there occur parables of varying degrees of "narrativity" and varying degrees of opacity. Moreover there is a relation between these properties: "narrativity" always entails a measure of opacity.

For the last century or so there has been something of a consensus among experts that parables of the kind found in the New Testament were always essentially simple, and always had the same kind of point, which would have been instantly taken by all listeners, outsiders included. Appearances to the contrary are explained as consequences of a process of meddling with the originals that began at the earliest possible moment. The opinion that the parables must originally have been thus, and only thus, is maintained with an expense of learning I can't begin to emulate, against what seems obvious, that "parable" does and did mean much more than that. When God says he will speak to Moses openly and not in "dark speeches," the Greek for "dark speeches" means "parables." John uses a different word for parable, but uses it in just the same sense: "speak in parables" is the opposite of "openly proclaim." If a word can cover so many things, from proverbial wisdom to dark sayings requiring recondite rabbinical explanation, and even to secret apocalyptic signs, it seems likely that people who used the word in this way must have interpreted all narrative with a comparable variety and range.

In our own time we cannot easily use the word "parable" in such a way as to exclude the notion of "enigma." Who would deny Kafka the right to call his anecdote of the leopards a parable (*Gleichnis*)? "Leopards break into the temple and drink to the dregs what is in the sacrificial pitchers; this is repeated over and over again; finally it can be calculated in advance, and it becomes part of the ceremony." Webster (third edition, 1961) says that a parable is "a short fictitious story from which a moral or spiritual truth can be drawn." Do we draw any such truth from Kafka's parable? What, to mention first a rather minor difficulty, are we to make of those definite articles: *the* temple, *the* sacrificial pitchers? They imply that the cultus is one with which we ought to be familiar; we ought to know the god whom the temple serves, and what liquid is contained in the pitchers. Of course we don't. All we can suppose is that some familiar rite is being intruded upon, and that the intrusion is assimilated, the cultus altered to accommodate it, in a manner often discussed by sociologists of religion. The alternative procedure, to their way of thinking, would be to shoot ("nihilate") the leopards.

Beyond that, we are left to consider the peculiar nature of the rite. There are ceremonies which claim to enact an historical sequence of events that occurred at a particularly significant moment in the past, and to do so in such a way as to translate them into the dimension of liturgy. The Passover is such a ceremony, and so is the Eucharist; both include expositions of the recurring symbolic senses of the original events. But here the repetitiveness belongs in the first place to the original events ("this is repeated over and over again") and only later becomes liturgical; though it might be argued that the presence of the leopards is all the more a Real Presence. At this point, it must be admitted, we are very close to what might be called "wild interpretation."

Here I will interpolate a reading of the parable by another hand, my wife's [Anita Kermode]. "The letter of the parable," she writes,

> masters our freedom to interpret it. The words, we know, must mean more and other than they say; we would appropriate their other sense. But the parable serenely incorporates our spiritual designs upon it. The interpreter may be compared to the greedy leopards. As their carnal intrusion is made spiritual, confirming the original design of the ceremony, so is this figurative reading pre-figured; only complying with the sense, it adds nothing of its own and takes nothing away. In comparing himself to the leopards, the reader finds himself, unlike the leopards, free—but free only to stay outside. Thus dispossessed by his own metaphor, excluded by his very desire for access, he repeatedly reads and fails to read the words that continue to say exactly what they mean.

This reading, which firmly excludes speculation about liturgy or ritual, has, I think, much to be said for it. Thurber, peering into a microscope, saw his own eye, which was wrong; interpreters, often quite rightly, tend to see the Problem of Interpretation. The sense of the parable, on the view just stated, must be this: being an insider is only a more elaborate way of being kept outside. This interpretation maintains that interpretation, though a proper and interesting activity, is bound to fail; it is an intrusion always, and always unsuccessful. This is bewildering, for we fear damnation and think it unfair, considering how hard we tried. The opinion of Mark is quite similar: he says that the parables are about everybody's incapacity to penetrate their sense. Of course both the interpreters in question go some way toward exempting themselves from this general inhibition.

There is a famous parable in Kafka's *The Trial*. It is recounted to K by a priest, and is said to come from the scriptures. A man comes and begs for admittance to the Law, but is kept out by a doorkeeper, the first of a long succession of doorkeepers, of aspect ever more terrible, who will keep the man out should the first one fail to do so. The man, who had assumed that the Law was open to all, is surprised to discover the existence of this arrangement. But he waits outside the door, sitting year after year on his stool, and conversing with the doorkeeper, whom he bribes, though without success. Eventually, when he is old and near death, the man observes an immortal radiance streaming from the door. As he dies, he asks the doorkeeper how it is that he alone has come to this entrance to seek admittance to the Law. The answer is, "This door was intended only for you. Now I am going to shut it." The outsider, though someone had "intended" to let him in, or anyway provided a door for him, remained outside.

K engages the priest in a discussion concerning the interpretation of this parable. He is continually reproved for his departures from the literal sense, and is offered a number of priestly glosses, all of which seem somehow trivial or absurd, unsatisfying or unfair, as when the doorkeeper is said to be more deserving of pity than the suppliant, since the suppliant was there of his own free will, as the porter was not. Nevertheless it is claimed that the doorkeeper belongs to the Law, and the man does not. K points out that to assume the integrity of the doorkeeper, or indeed that of the Law, as the priest does, involves contradictions. No, replies the priest: "It is not necessary to accept everything as true, one must only accept it as necessary." "A melancholy conclusion," says K. "It turns lying into a universal principle."

"Before the Law" is a good deal longer than any biblical parable, and reminds us that in principle parable may escape restrictions of length, and be, say, as long as *Party Going*. And like Mark's parable of the Sower, it incorporates very dubious interpretations, which help to make the point that the would-be interpreter cannot get inside, cannot even properly dispose of authoritative interpretations that are more or less obviously wrong. The outsider has what appears to be a reasonable, normal, and just expectation of ready admittance, for the Law, like the Gospel, is meant for everybody, or everybody who wants it. But what he gets is a series of frivolous and mendacious interpretations. The outsider remains outside, dismayed and frustrated. To perceive the radiance of the shrine is not to gain access to it; the Law, or the kingdom, may, to those within, be powerful and beautiful, but to those outside they are merely terrible; absolutely inexplicable, they torment the inquirer with legalisms. This is a mystery; Mark, and Kafka's doorkeeper, protect it without understanding it, and those outside, like K and like us, see an uninterpretable radiance and die.

Let me now return to Mark's formula of exclusion, which I quoted near the beginning of the book. Jesus is preaching to a crowd, teaching them "many things in parables." The first is the parable of the Sower. He went out to sow; some of his seed fell by the wayside and was eaten by birds; some fell on stony ground, where it grew without rooting and was scorched by the sun; some fell among thorns, which choked it; and some fell on good ground, yielding at harvest thirty, sixty, and a hundredfold. "He that hath ears to hear, let him hear": this is the formula that tells you the enigmatic part of the text is concluded, and you need to start interpreting. Later, the twelve, baffled, ask Jesus what the parable means. He replies that they, his elect, know the mystery of the kingdom and do not need to be addressed in parables, but those outside are addressed only thus, "*so that* seeing they may see and not perceive, and hearing they may hear but not understand, *lest* at any time they should turn, and their sins be forgiven them" (Mark 4:11–12). He adds, a little crossly, that if the twelve can't make out this parable they will not make out any of them, but nevertheless goes on to give them an interpretation. What the Sower sows is the Word. People by the wayside hear it, but Satan (the birds) comes and takes it from their hearts. The stony ground signifies those who receive the Word with gladness, but are unable to retain it under stress and persecution; the thorns stand for those who hear it but allow it to be choked by worldly lust and ambition. The last group are those who hear and receive the Word and bear much fruit (4:14–20).

All this is very odd; the authorized allegory seems inept, a distortion *après coup,* as bad as the priest's exegeses in Kafka. It gives rise to suggestions that Mark did not understand the parable, that its original sense was already lost, and its place taken by an inferior homiletic substitute. But let us put that question aside and look at the general theory of parable pronounced on this occasion: To you has been given the secret of the kingdom of God, but for those outside everything is in parables, so that they may indeed see but not perceive, and may hear but not understand; lest they should turn again and be forgiven. Some argue that Mark's *so that* or *in order that,* the Greek *hina,* is a mistranslation of a word that in the last Aramaic original meant *in that* or *in such a manner as,* so that Mark's Greek distorts the true sense, which is something like: I have to speak to them in parables, seeing that they are the kind of people who can take stories but not straight doctrine. This is an attempt to make *hina* mean "because," a very desirable state of affairs. In this altered form the theory no longer conflicts with the prefatory remark that Jesus was *teaching* the crowd, which seems inconsistent with his telling stories in order to ensure that they would miss the point. It also fits the run of the sentence better: the twelve don't need parables, but the crowd does. Apparently Mark misunderstood, or used *hina* carelessly or in an unusual way; and it is a fairly complex word. But the best authorities do not accept these evasive explanations, a refusal all the more impressive because they would really like to. They admit that Mark's *hina* has to mean *in order that;* and we are left with a doctrine described by one standard modern commentator as "intolerable," by Albert Schweitzer as "repellent," and also, since the meaning of the parables is "as clear as day," unintelligible.

Now it happens that Mark's first interpreter was Matthew (I assume throughout that Mark has priority and is Matthew's principal source, though this long-established position is now under challenge). And Matthew also seems to have found Mark's *hina* intolerable. For though he does not omit the general theory of parable from his big parable chapter 13, he substitutes for *hina* the word *hoti,* "because." This is a substantial change, involving a different grammar; Matthew replaces Mark's subjunctive with an indicative. Later he had to deal with Mark's *mēpote,* "*lest* they should turn," which obviously supports the uncompromising mood of *hina;* here he went to work in a different way. The whole passage about hearing and seeing comes from Isaiah (6:9–10), though Mark, in paraphrasing it, does not say so. What Matthew does is to quote Isaiah directly and with acknowledgment, so that the lines retain a trace of their original tone of slightly disgusted irony at the failure of the people to perceive and understand. The sense is now something like: As Isaiah remarked, their stupidity is extremely tiresome; this seems the best way to get through to them. The *mēpote* clause is thus bracketed off from the rest; instead of Mark's uncompromising exclusions—outsiders must stay outside and be damned—Matthew proposes something much milder: "I speak to them in parables *because* they see without perceiving. . . ." He was, it appears, unhappy with the gloomy ferocity of Mark's Jesus, who is also, in this place, very hard on the twelve: "If you don't understand this you won't understand anything." Matthew leaves this out, and substitutes a benediction: "Blessed are your eyes, for they see. . . ."

It has been argued that Matthew's *hoti* has a causal force, that he is saying something like: It is only because the people lack understanding that the parables will have the effect of keeping them from the secrets of the kingdom. The implication is that the exclusion arises not from the speaker's intention, but from the stupidity of his hearers, so that the blame is theirs. This gives the parables the same effect as they have in Mark's theory, while avoiding his candid avowal that the telling of them was designed to have that effect. I must leave *hoti's* business to the grammarians, but it seems safe to say that Matthew's principle of secret and inaccessible senses, if he had one, is a good deal softer than Mark's. When he came to edit Mark's concluding note ("he said nothing to them without a parable," 4:34) Matthew adds that Jesus in so doing was fulfilling the Psalmist's prophecy: "I will open my mouth in parables, I will utter what has been hidden since the foundation of the world" (Matt. 13:34–35; Ps. 78:2). And in support of this preference for overt proclamation, Matthew omits the remainder of Mark's sentence quoted above: "But privately to his own disciples he explained everything." *Ereugomai,* the verb translated as "utter" in Matthew's quotation, means "disgorge, vomit forth, spew out" and can only suggest total disclosure. On the other hand, it is Matthew who remarks, at the moment when he is explaining the difference between insiders and outsiders (13:12) that "to him who has will more be given . . . but from him who has not, even what he has will be taken away," a saying used by Mark later on in the parallel chapter, and in a different context. So Matthew's position is hard to define, though we can say it was less intransigent than Mark's. It is sometimes suggested that from this moment of the ministry Jesus has given up trying to get himself understood by the Jews, whom he therefore does not mind baffling. Whether this is true or not, we can say we have two kindred but different secrecy theories. Each of them makes the parable a bit like a riddle in a folktale, where to get the answer wrong means perdition;

but *hina* and *hoti* distinguish them. One says the stories are obscure on purpose to damn the outsiders; the other, even if we state it in the toughest form the language will support, says that they are not necessarily impenetrable, but that the outsiders, being what they are, will misunderstand them anyway.

Now if you think that Jesus could not possibly have thought of his parables as riddles designed to exclude the masses from the kingdom; and if you have also the prior knowledge that the original parables cannot have been allegorical—so that, quite apart from this particular allegory being so feeble, you know it should not be there at all—then you are virtually obliged to claim that the whole Marcan passage is inauthentic or corrupt. Since A. Jülicher set the tone of modern parable criticism at the end of the nineteenth century, this has been the general view. According to Jülicher, Mark simply misunderstood the parable as he had it from the tradition. There are many explanations of how he might have come to do so; but behind them all is a conviction that the parables must originally have been simple illustrations of the teacher's point, made in order to help those who had difficulty with abstractions. The purpose of the Sower parable, as many think, was, like that of most of the parables, eschatological: it had to do with the end-time that had now come upon the world, with the breaking-in of the kingdom of God, here represented by the harvest, a traditional figure for it. Between sowing and harvest many frustrations occur; but when the harvest comes, and the angel puts in his sickle, all will be fruition and triumph. For this original, Jewish, eschatological sense, Mark substitutes his feeble, Hellenistic, homiletic allegory. His theory of impenetrable narrative darkness is likewise an error. Jesus occasionally made despairing observations, and Mark, somehow misled, took this one from its proper place and attached it to a group of parables with which it has nothing whatever to do.

One can't help thinking of Kafka's parables as recalling these clerical contentions. Kafka, like Mark, or the text of Mark as we have it, supports what might be called the *hina* doctrine of narrative. The desire to change *hina* to *hoti* is a measure of the dismay we feel at our arbitrary and total exclusion from the kingdom, or from secret sense of the story, of which we learn—by its radiance—only that it is overwhelmingly important. Both Mark and Kafka go on to offer unacceptable priestly glosses on their parables. Each seems to arrive at a melancholy conclusion. Matthew took the first step toward reducing the bleak mystery of Mark's proposals; and later a rational, scientific scholarship spirited away the enigma by detecting behind the text of Mark a version more to its liking.

Of course what the scholars say is plausible. They speak of a redactor living after the time when the kingdom was imminently expected, so that he had lost the original eschatological sense of the story. He remodeled it in such a way that its original meaning was muddled by an incongruous interpretation. The attempts of the learned to explain away Mark's *hina* are worthy of Kafka's priest. But there it stands, and has stood for nineteen hundred years, a silent proclamation that stories can always be enigmatic, and can sometimes be terrible. And Mark's Gospel as a whole—to put the matter too simply—is either enigmatic and terrible, or as muddled as the commentators say this passage is. Why, to ask a famous question, does Mark so stress the keeping of the secret of the messiahship of Jesus? One answer is that since this was an idea that developed only after the death of Jesus, Mark was forced to include it in his narrative *only* as a secret deliberately kept, concealed from all save the twelve, and not understood by them until the end of the story. This leaves a good deal unexplained; nor is the theme of secrecy the only mystery in Mark. My present point is simple enough: Mark is a strong witness to the enigmatic and exclusive character of narrative, to its property of banishing interpreters from its secret places. He could say *hina*, even though his ostensible purpose, as declared in the opening words of his book, was the proclamation of good news to all.

The Sower parable is the great crux. But it is not a parable that has any of the expansiveness or expressiveness of a short story; and it first occurs in the most difficult of the Gospel texts. The Good Samaritan is an example of parable as extended narrative; and it occurs only in Luke (10:25–37), who is generally thought of as the most literary as well as the most genial and bourgeois of the evangelists. I will use it to comment on varieties of interpretation, and on the division between those who suppose that all stories have obscure senses and those who think this need not be so.

All the synoptics have the episode in which a lawyer or scribe asks Jesus which is the greatest commandment, though Luke changes the question to "What shall I do to inherit eternal life?" In Mark (12:28–34) and Matthew (22:34–40) the answer is an unadorned declaration of the requirement to love God and one's neighbor; Mark adds that Jesus commended the lawyer for knowing that obedience to these commandments was more important than burnt offerings and sacrifices.

Luke again varies the procedure; instead of answering the lawyer's question, Jesus puts one of his own: "What is written in the law? How do you read?" Luke accepts the hint that the lawyer is testing Jesus; Mark does not say so, and indeed his report is inconsistent with the notion of a contest. Such contests often breed parables; so Luke includes one. When the lawyer gets the answer right, Jesus tells him so. But the lawyer, desiring to justify himself, said to Jesus, "And who is my neighbor?"

The answer to this question is the parable. According to Luke, it is meant to explain the sense of the word "neighbor" (*plēsion*). Naturally, being a coherent narrative, it says more than is strictly necessary to make this point. (The obligation upon narratives to do this is, by the way, a great generator of narrative senses.) A traveler is robbed and left wounded in a ditch. A priest and a Levite pass by without offering assistance, but a third passerby goes to much trouble and expense to help the victim. He is a Samaritan—a member, that is, of a nation hated and despised by the Jews. The nature of his help is specified: he binds up the wounds, treats them with oil and wine, carries the half-dead patient on his own beast to an inn, and, having left with the innkeeper a supply of money for further care, departs with a promise to return. Which of the three travelers proved neighbor to the wounded man?

Here is a narrative that seems to be a simple exemplary tale. The detail that could be called redundant to its merely exemplary purpose may be explained away as a gesture toward realism, a way of adding the interest of verisimilitude, or even of topicality, to the folktalish triple design of the story. The Jericho road is chosen because it was a road on which such assaults were frequent. The Samaritan does all that can be done to help the man, expending his supplies, forfeiting the use of his animal, giving the innkeeper a precisely specified sum of money (enough to cater for the man's needs over many days) and, so far from thinking that he had now discharged his neighborly duty, promising to come back and finish the good work. This is how one ought to behave *now*, not in some storybook situation that vaguely impends. Perhaps the point is being made with such determined clarity because *we* need help, and ought not to be left in a ditch of incomprehension.

Yet this simple view of the story is very far from having gained universal acceptance. And in understanding why this is so we happen upon an important, if obvious, reason for the interminability of interpretation. My way of reading the detail of the parable of the Good

Samaritan seems to me natural; but that is only my way of authenticating, or claiming as universal, a habit of thought that is cultural and arbitrary. My reading would certainly not have seemed "natural" to the church fathers, for instance. The Holy Ghost does not give details merely to please or reassure; in all his works every word and every figure is charged with sense. The fate of the traveler represents the fall of the human race into the hands of demons; he is Adam, who has left Jerusalem, the heavenly city, for Jericho, the world. The Samaritan is Christ, the inn is the Church, the promise to return the Second Coming.

To such interpreters the story is loaded with hidden meanings and although there will be a consensus as to certain of these, there is no suggestion that the process of interpretation need ever cease. The reading I've just alluded to is that of Irenaeus. A Gnostic allegorist proposed that the wine and oil embody an esoteric conception of *chrisma*. Augustine interpreted the parable on several occasions, with some variation. The main purpose of the parable is to show the continuing care of the Samaritan (which means "Keeper"); for although all sins are remitted by baptism (the wine and oil) man is still weak, must be lifted up, tended and strengthened at the inn, which is the Church. Or, more elaborately, the wounded man is Adam, who has left heaven for the world (Jericho means the moon, the sphere of mutability) and fallen into the hands of demons, who strip him of immortality, leaving him half-dead. The priest and Levite represent the inefficacious old dispensation, the oil is hope and the wine good works; the beast is representative of the Incarnation, the inn of the Church, and the innkeeper of the apostle Paul. This interpretation, as Dodd remarks, had great authority and longevity; but it was always subject to variation, the inexhaustibility of the text being greater than the authority even of Augustine. No doubt the parable has a carnal sense which does not vary materially; its spiritual sense in not so constant.

And we should reflect that interpretations of the kind I have touched upon were applied to narratives other than parables. All narrative is susceptible. For example, Augustine, interpreting the five loaves and two fishes of the first Feeding, says that the loaves are the books of Moses—they are of barley, rough outside and hard to open, but containing much nourishment; while the fish represent Christ in his characters as Priest and King. The multiplication of the loaves is the exposition of the Law in many volumes. The number of thousands of people is five because the people were under Mosaic Law. They sat on the grass because, being carnally minded, they rested on sensual things. The fragments they left were truths of hidden import, such as they were unable to receive (they took the carnal, left the spiritual). And so on.

The persistence of this kind of explanation is well known; the following interpretation of the same passage was written more than a thousand years later:

> By the five loaves, doctors understand the five Books of Moses which are aptly compared to a barley loaf; for a barley loaf on its outside is rough, in part, and harsh . . . yet within it is full of the purest flour . . . By the two fishes are signified the Prophets and Psalms, and the book of the Apocalypse in the New Testament, which, taken in their literal sense, are more difficult and obscure than the aforesaid books, but none the less in their mystical senses are far more fruitful. So it is with the Gospels and the Canonical Epistles of Paul; for as fishes lie hid in the waters, so the moral senses lurk hidden in these books.

Or the five loaves are the five wounds of Christ; the two fishes are the Virgin Mary and the penitent thief; the twelve baskets are the twelve articles of the Creed or the Twelve Apostles—"whichever you like," adds the preacher, certain that liberty of interpreting exists, though doubtless not without constraint. I mention these medieval variations to illustrate a point made [elsewhere]: . . . an institutional tradition—such as that which transmitted Augustine's interpretation to medieval preachers—does not inhibit the indefinite multiplication of spiritual readings. One divination spawns another. If I say the fishes are one thing, that does not prevent your saying they are another, just as plausibly; and you may tell me, with notable liberality, that I may make them stand for anything I choose, though there will be a family or institutional resemblance between our interpretations.

Later the admissibility of such readings became an important issue in hermeneutics. There had long been a literalist opposition to free allegory, but Luther's rejection of it was decisive, and in the era of "scientific" interpretation it was rejected absolutely. Yet science also makes its assumptions. For example, it was assumed that the parable of the Good Samaritan existed before Luke wrote it down (an assumption now challenged, and for which there is no evidence). And of course Luke was accused to getting it wrong.

It is true that good sense may be made of Luke's version if we supply some historical context. For instance, the question "Who is my friend?" was less vague than it now sounds; certain rules of caste and race were involved. Also, by the folktale rule of three, you expect a third passerby. Since the first two were an Israelite priest and a Levite, you might also expect that the third will be an Israelite layman—that the story, written at a time when the clergy were greatly disliked, will turn out to be anticlerical. However, by a rather shocking peripeteia, the third man turns out to be an enemy and unclean. So the story, instead of saying that lay folk can be more charitable than parsons, a commonplace truth, extends the sense of *plēsion* quite violently to include the least likely person imaginable, and so, by implication, everybody.

This seems reasonable, but narrative is not a very reasonable subject, and the view that this tale, however transparent it may seem, however self-sufficient, *must* have senses less obvious than that is certainly not extinct. One modern interpreter argues that the surface, with its blend of reassuring local detail and folktale, conceals a sense that depends on secret allusion to a repertory of Old Testament texts. That such repertories existed is not in doubt, and I shall refer to them later. The argument in this case is that so far from merely illustrating the second commandment, the story of the Samaritan is about the Second coming. "Samaritan" (as Augustine seems to have known) comes from the same root as "shepherd"; the Samaritan is the Good Shepherd. Moreover, *plēsion,* neighbor, is related to another Hebrew word meaning "shepherd"; and the original parable, now concealed by Luke's, asked "Who is the true shepherd?" So the lawyer asked a new question and got the answer to an old one: the Good Shepherd, who comforts our distress and will return hereafter. This "futuristic" eschatology is wholly lost in Luke's hortatory conclusion, "go and do likewise." But science enables us to recover the true sense, already imperceptible to Luke. It happens to be quite close to the sense proposed by the Fathers I've referred to, but the method is of course quite different, theirs being allegorical and this being scientific. Other scientific readings bear no resemblance to patristic allegory: for example, the argument that the parable was written to justify sending a mission to Samaria.

I suppose we could say that none of these interpretations leaves the parable untouched, unintruded upon, though it is easy to see that some regard it as deeply enigmatic and some do not. Those who think it enigmatic also think they can explain the enigma rather fully, as Augustine did long ago, and as Gerhardsson did only a few years back when he identified the Samaritan with the Good Shepherd. Gerhardsson says, in effect, that what he has unearthed *is* the interpretation. However, there is a fashion still more recent, which revives, in its own way, the notion that the sense of the text is inexhaustibly occult, and accessible in a different form to each and every interpreter. The object of this kind of interpretation is no longer "scientific"; one does not try, like Jeremias, to state what the narrative meant in its original, or in any later setting; one does not try to "re-cognize" it, as the more conservative hermeneutical theorists say one should. Rather one assumes, to quote an opponent of this school, that "the meaning of a text goes beyond its author not sometimes but always" and that "one understands differently when one understands at all." The object of interpretation is now sometimes said to be to retrieve, if necessary by benign violence, what is called the original event of disclosure. This is the language of Heidegger; he takes the Greek word for "truth," *alētheia*, in its etymological sense, "that which is revealed or disclosed, does not remain concealed." Every hermeneutic encounter with a text is an encounter with Being as disclosed in it. For Heidegger indeed, it is the very fact that one is *outside* that makes possible the revelation of truth or meaning; being *inside* is like being in Plato's cave.

Every such hermeneutic encounter is still, in a measure, historically conditioned, though now that limitation is no longer thought of just as a limitation—it is the prerequisite of interpretation, each act of which is unique, one man on one stool, so to speak, seeing what no power can withhold from him, his glimpse of the radiance, his share of what is sometimes called the "hermeneutic potential" of a text. Interpreters in this tradition sometimes think of earlier interpretations, transmitted by institutions, as having attached themselves to the original, and as having tended to close it off, lowering its potential rather as mineral deposits clog a pipe and reduce its flow. Since by their own interpretative act they discover what the parable *originally means*, they are not constricted by the conventional demand that interpretation should say what the parable *originally meant*, to its author and its first audience. What it meant and what it means are both actualizations of its hermeneutic potential, which, though never fully available, is inexhaustible.

Now that which requires to be disclosed must first have been covered, and this view of interpretation certainly implies that the sense of the parable is an occult sense. Its defenders like to say not that the interpreter illumines the text, but that the text illumines the interpreter, like a radiance. For this, as I said, is an outsider's theory. It stems ultimately from a Protestant tradition, that of the devout dissenter animated only by the action of the Spirit, abhorring the claim of the institution to a historically validated traditional interpretation. It may be the end of that tradition; for I do not see how, finally, it can distinguish between sacred and secular texts, those works of the worldly canon that also appear to possess inexhaustible hermeneutic potential. (Heidegger's own exegeses of Hölderlin treat the text exactly as if it were sacred.) The tradition is that of a productive encounter between the text and the reader, illuminated by a peculiar grace or, in more secular terms, a divinatory genius, as far as possible independent of institutional or historical control. That encounter is the main concern not only of modern German hermeneutics but also, though their ways are different, of its French rivals. The method has, of course, been applied to the parables.

An interpreter working in this tradition cannot altogether free himself from historical and institutional constraints. He will try to avoid them, insofar as they are avoidable; but he cannot escape his own historicality, and he was trained in an institution. Nor can he acquire divinatory genius for the asking. The book that first made American readers familiar with the idea of hermeneutic potential was Robert Funk's *Language, Hermeneutic, and the Word of God.* It is an admirable piece of exposition. Yet Funk agrees with Jeremias that the effect of the Good Samaritan story depends on the narrative shock of the discovery that the merciful traveler is a stranger, an enemy. He departs from known paths only when he conjectures that the wounded man might have preferred not to have the assistance of this unclean outcast; but this is a conjecture that owes nothing to the new hermeneutics. Although he denies the Good Shepherd interpretation, he agrees that Jesus is the Samaritan, and we the wounded man; so the Good Shepherd is there somewhere, in a sort of penumbra. There seems to be a traditional quality about this reading that is rather remote from the libertarian possibilities suggested by the speculative parts of Funk's book, and very remote from the unique and somber meditations of Heidegger on Hölderlin.

This is perhaps to say no more than that the interpreter is likely to have a touch of the dyer's hand. Thus structuralist exegesis of this parable will pass from a demonstration of its narrativity to a demonstration that Luke, as many have said before, mistook a parable of the Kingdom for a homiletic example story. And Paul Ricoeur is surely right to assume that interpretation begins where structuralist analysis ends, that such analysis should be thought of as a way of facilitating divination.

I take it that the Good Samaritan sufficiently illustrates the point that a story need not be manifestly obscure to be thought by interpreters to possess that which only interpretation may disclose. I will end with a word on another parable, partly to accustom us to the existence of variants in gospel narrative, partly to make a point about allegorical interpretation that I have not had time to develop.

The parable of the Wicked Husbandmen occurs in all three synoptic Gospels, and in all three it follows a contest between Jesus and the chief priests or scribes and elders on the topic of his authority, for which he refuses explanations. The connection between the parable and this dispute is not obvious; there may not be one. Moreover the three versions differ significantly. Mark's is quite circumstantial: a man plants a vineyard, surrounded by a hedge and containing a tower and a winepress. Then he lets it to tenants and leaves the country. On his return he sends a servant to demand some of the fruit, presumably in accordance with the original contract. The tenants beat the servant and send him away. So he sends another, who is even worse treated, and then a third, whom the tenants kill, and then more, all of whom are either beaten or killed. Finally the landlord sends his only son (or his beloved son—the same word serves for both), supposing that the tenants will at least respect him. But they kill him too, hoping thereby to inherit the estate. What, in such circumstances, will the landlord do? He will come and destroy the tenants and give the vineyard to others (Mark 12:1–9).

This is a somewhat implausible narrative, but Matthew's variations (21:33–44) are not designed to help it in this respect. He develops the ending, saying that the new tenants will be of the kind who will ungrudgingly give up a proper share of the fruit; and he makes an explicit application: "The kingdom of God will be taken away from you and given to a nation producing the fruits of it" (21:43). He makes another change which I will mention later. Luke cuts out the tower, the winepress, and the hedge, and sends only three servants in advance of the son; they are maltreated but not killed, which improves the progression of the tale (20:9–18). The simplest and most elegant version is in the apocryphal Gospel of Thomas, a volume in the Gnostic library discovered at Nag Hamadi in Upper Egypt some thirty years ago (Logion 65). Thomas sends only two servants, who are beaten; then the son, who is killed. Thomas, who never appends interpretations, says nothing about the reaction of the father. In the present instance the synoptics also withhold direct interpretation, though all add, more or less clumsily, the saying about the stone that the builders rejected, which yet became the cornerstone.

The parable of the Wicked Husbandmen looks very like an allegory, which is why the first reaction of scientific criticism was to regard it as inauthentic, as something made up in the church and read back into the gospel account. Let us suppose that there lies behind it a simple tale, very like Thomas's version. There were three emissaries, the first two beaten and the third killed. Having lost his property and his son, the landlord is now obliged to do something decisive; the synoptics give their versions of what this was. Mark has muddled this simple scenario. He sends not three but an indefinite number of messengers, and fails to make the treatment they receive more and more severe. And he puts in a good deal of unmistakably allegorical detail. The winepress, the tower, and the hedge come from Isaiah (5:1–2) where they are already allegorical; the vineyard is Israel. And when Mark describes the last messenger as the *huios agapētos* (beloved or only son) of the lord, he cannot be forgetting that he makes God use exactly these words of Jesus at the opening of his book (*Su ei ho huios mou ho agapētos,* 1:11). The allegory is now plain: God sent his prophets to Israel (not only two of them, hence the greater number of messengers); they were abused by the Israelites or their rulers; then he sent his son and they killed him, too. (This presupposes, on the part of Jesus, a foreknowledge of his own death, which is one reason why the scientific critics regard the parable as inauthentic.)

Matthew of course saw the point, and developed it. Where Mark says the son was killed, then cast out of the vineyard, Matthew says he was cast out and then killed; the Crucifixion took place outside the city wall. Luke cares less for allegory, dropping the Isaian tower; but he uses Matthew's order, first casting out, then slaying. Thomas alone shuns all allegory, contenting himself with the formulaic "Whoever has ears let him hear." But this is perhaps no more than an invitation to do the allegory yourself, if you can.

So it seems that the parable is an allegory, and has no point except as an allegory. It is more like Spenser's House of Holiness than Kafka's Leopards in the Temple. The reason why Mark put in a lot of messengers was simply that there had been a lot of prophets; to have only *three* would have obscured this point. Spenser represents the Seven Corporal Works of Mercy by seven beadsmen, not three. But if it *is* an allegory, where should licit allegorization stop? The common patristic answer is, of course, nowhere. Allegory is the patristic way of dealing with inexhaustible hermeneutic potential. And the Fathers had many successors; the notion that ancient myth as well as Scripture concealed occult wisdom was as common during the European Renaissance as it was in the Hellenistic world. By contrast later scholars ask only what kind of allegory one may expect the evangelists to have inserted into a story that was not in itself allegorical at all. Then they ask what the story meant in its original form, before the salvation allegory got attached to it. Jülicher simply rejects the whole thing as inauthentic. Jeremias and Dodd say it reflects the resentment felt by Galilean tenant farmers toward their absentee foreign landlords; such landlords might, when all else failed, send their sons to collect, and the tenants might kill them in the hope of benefiting from a law that assigned ownerless property to the first claimant. They were wrong to do so, of course, and God would give the vineyard not to them but to the poor. But this is only a more rationalistic allegory; it denies that the parable was originally what it certainly later became, a prophecy of the Crucifixion, and turns it into a somewhat ridiculous fable about current affairs.

In fact it seems impossible to think of the tale appearing in the gospel context simply as a tale. So the difficulty (unless we take the dissentient view that the parable as we have it is much as it always was) is merely that different interpretations have got attached in the course of time to the same parable. Paul Ricoeur thinks of interpretation as the linking of a new discourse to the discourse of the text; in a sense he treats the formal description of a narrative (as by the structuralists) as carnal, the long historical succession of interpretations as spiritual: the "form" of a parable (that which can be analyzed in terms of internal synchronic relations) is what ensures the survival of meaning after the disappearance of the original historical setting; and that meaning arises form a kind of conversation between the interpreter and the text. A parable, he says, is a fiction capable of redescribing life; its sense can never be fully closed, or this process of redescription would not be possible. It is, one might add, a paradox applying to all narrative that although its function is mnemonic it always recalls different things. The mode of recall will depend in some measure on the fashion of a period—what it seems natural or reasonable to expect a text to say. This is another way of affirming that all narratives possess "hermeneutic potential," which is another way of saying that they must be obscure. The apparently perspicuous narrative yields up latent senses to interpretation; we are never inside it, and from the outside may never experience anything more than some radiant intimation of the source of all these senses.

So inveterate, so unalterable is this exclusion that it is easy to pass from saying that the outsiders are told stories because they are dull and imperceptive to saying that stories are told in order to keep the dull and imperceptive outside. And suppose that we somehow discovered that all stories were, after all, *hoti* stories. The interpreters *de métier* would, to protect their profession, to continue their privileged conversations with texts, at once strive to discredit the discovery; finally all stories are *hina* stories, even the story that they are all *hoti*.

That all narratives are essentially dark, despite the momentary radiance that attends divination, is a doctrine that would not have surprised prescientific interpreters. They might have offered various reasons for holding it, though usually they would have attributed the darkness of the tale to the intention of a divine author. Calvin and Pascal, close as they were to the epoch in which a presumptuous human reason would attempt to explain the mystery away, nevertheless agreed with Mark that the divine author made his stories obscure in order to prevent the reprobate from understanding them; on a kinder Catholic view, he did so in order to minimize the guilt of the Jews in refusing the Gospel. Even now, when so many theories of interpretation dispense in one way or another with the author, or allow him only a part analogous to that of the dummy hand at bridge, the position is not much altered; the narrative inhabits its proper dark, in which the interpreter traces its lineaments as best he can. Kafka, whose interpreter dies outside, is a doorkeeper only; so was Mark.

Mark distresses the commentators by using the word "mystery" as a synonym for "parable," and assuming that stories put questions which even the most privileged interpreters cannot answer. For example, he tells two stories about miraculous Feedings (Mark 6:35–44; 8:1–9). Any creative writing instructor would have cut one of them; but Mark's awkwardness can hardly be dismissed as accidental. Later the disciples are on board a boat and discover that they have forgotten to bring bread—there is only one loaf. At this point Jesus gives them an obscure warning: "Beware of the leaven of the Pharisees and the leaven of Herod" (Mark 8:15). Puzzled, they say among themselves, "It is because we have no bread," or "This is why we have no bread," or, maybe, "Is this why we have no bread?"—the sense of the Greek is uncertain. Whatever they intend, Jesus gets angry. "Do you not yet perceive or understand? Are your hearts hardened? Having eyes do you not see, and having ears do you not hear?" They are behaving exactly like the outsiders in the theory of parable. The sign given them by the Feedings is lost on them, and unless something is done about it they will find themselves in the same position as the Pharisees, to whom Jesus has just refused any sign at all. So he takes them once more, slowly, through the story of the Feedings. Five thousand were fed with five loaves: how many baskets of fragments were left over? Twelve, they correctly reply. Four thousand, at the second Feeding, were served with seven loaves: how many baskets of fragments were left over? Seven. Well then, don't you see the point? Silence. Perhaps the disciples mistook the riddle as we do the one about the elephants: there is a strong suggestion that the answer has to do with number, but it probably doesn't. Anyway, they do not find the answer. Here again Matthew does not want to leave the matter so obscure; his Jesus is much less reproachful, and also explains: "How did you fail to see that I was not talking about bread? Beware of the leaven of the Pharisees and Sadducees." ("Leaven," used figuratively, ordinarily meant something infectiously evil.) "Then they understood that he was not telling them to beware of the leaven of bread, but of the teaching of the Pharisees and Sadducees" (16:12). This is not perhaps very satisfactory; but the point is that Mark, with his usual severity, makes Jesus angry and disappointed, and also turns the insiders into outsiders. They cannot answer this riddle, any more than they could read the parable of the Sower. And although this passage has been subjected to the intense scrutiny of the commentators, no one, so far as I know, has improved on the disciples' performance. The riddle remains dark; so does the Gospel.

Parable, it seems, may proclaim a truth as a herald does, and at the same time conceal truth like an oracle. This double function, this simultaneous proclamation and concealment, will be a principal theme of what follows [elsewhere], for I shall concern myself with the radiant obscurity of narratives somewhat longer than parables, though still subject to these Hermetic ambivalences.

Prophecy and the Gospel

Northrop Frye

The Gospel is a further intensifying of the prophetic vision. That vision, we suggested [elsewhere], had two levels: the level of the present moment and a level above it. The latter is both that of the original identity symbolized by the Garden of Eden (along with, as we shall see, the Promised Land and the Temple), and the ultimate identity symbolized by the return to these things after the "Day of the Lord" and the restoring of Israel. Jesus' teaching centers on the conception of a present spiritual kingdom that includes all these upper-level images, and on earth he is thought of as living simultaneously in it and among us.

To express this there have to be secondary metaphors of "descending" from the higher level, or "heaven," and of "ascending" back into it again. Prophecies of the restoration of Israel such as Isaiah's prophecy of Emmanuel in Isaiah 7, and Ezekiel's vision of the valley of dry bones in Ezekiel 37, were interpreted by Christians as types of the Incarnation or the Resurrection. Paul's brilliant phrase for the Incarnation is "He emptied himself" (Philippians 2:7; the Authorized Version's rendering is not a translation but an inept gloss). That is, he "descended" or was born into the world of vanity or total emptiness. The return to the spiritual world is "resurrection," a conception which, though it is a return from death, can hardly be confined to the revival of a dead body in a tomb. Jesus sometimes speaks of his central

From *The Great Code: The Bible and Literature.* © 1981, 1982 by Northrop Frye. Harcourt Brace Jovanovich, Inc., 1981.

doctrine of a spiritual kingdom as a mystery, a secret imparted to his disciples (though they often got it wrong too), with those outside the initiated group being put off with parables (Mark 4:11). It seems clear, however, that the real distinction between initiated and uninitiated is between those who think of achieving the spiritual kingdom as a way of life and those who understand it merely as a doctrine.

The way of life is described as beginning in *metanoia*, a word translated "repentance" by the Authorized Version, which suggests a moralized inhibition of the "stop doing everything you want to do" variety. What the word primarily means, however, is change of outlook or spiritual metamorphosis, an enlarged vision of the dimensions of human life. Such a vision, among other things, detaches one from one's primary community and attaches him to another. When John the Baptist says, "Bring forth fruits worthy of *metanoia*" (Matt. 3:8), he is addressing Jews, and goes on to say that their primary social identity (descent from Abraham) is of no spiritual importance. What one repents of is sin, a word that means nothing outside a religious and individualized context. That is, sin is not illegal or antisocial behavior. The "deadly" or mortal sins that destroy the soul were classified in the Middle Ages as pride, wrath, sloth, envy, avarice, gluttony, and lechery; and of these, heavily moralized as they are, not one necessarily results in criminal or antisocial acts. Sin is rather a matter of trying to block the activity of God, and it always results in some curtailing of human freedom, whether of oneself or of one's neighbor.

The dialectic of *metanoia* and sin splits the world into the kingdom of genuine identity, presented as Jesus' "home," and a hell, a conception found in the Old Testament only in the form of death or the grave. Hell is that, but it is also the world of anguish and torment that man goes on making for himself all through history. Jesus describes it in imagery of an undying worm and an unquenched fire, taken from the last verse of Isaiah, which speaks of the dead bodies of those overthrown in the final *culbute*. As a form of vision, *metanoia* reverses our usual conceptions of time and space. The central points of time and space are now and here, neither of which exists in ordinary experience. In ordinary experience "now" continually vanishes between the no longer and the not yet; we may think of "here" as a hazy mental circumference around ourselves, but whatever we locate in ordinary space, inside it or outside it, is "there" in a separated alien world. In the "kingdom" the eternal and infinite are not time and space made endless (they *are* endless already) but are the now and the here made real, an actual present and an actual presence. Time vanishes in Jesus' "Before Abraham was, I am" (John 8:58); space vanishes when we are told, in an aphorism previously referred to, that the kingdom is *entos hymon* (Luke 17:21), which may mean among you or in you, but in either case means here, not there.

In its relation to the previous phrases, the Gospel of *metanoia* makes man a "new creature" (2 Cor. 5:17), in which the original and now fallen order of nature becomes a mother bringing to birth a re-creation made through a union of God and man (Rom. 8:21). It is the reappearance in human life of the higher or transfigured nature, the innocent world before the Fall. The revolutionary thrust of the Exodus is also preserved, and Jesus often speaks of "faith" as though it gave the individual as much effective power as the Exodus gave the whole society of Israel. Such faith clearly includes a power of action informed by a vision transcending time and space. In the Old Testament law and wisdom follow the deliverance from Egypt. The totalitarian conception of the law, in which the breaker of an obligation to God is to be wiped out with his family (Josh. 7:24), had already given way to the principle that the individual alone was responsible for what he did (Ezek. 18:20). One of the pseudepigrapha, 2 Baruch, speaks of the law among us and the wisdom within us (48:24). But the Gospel is a different kind of individualizing of the law, founded on the category of prophecy. We remarked earlier that Christianity thinks of the Old Testament as primarily a book of prophecy rather than of law; and the principle involved here needs careful stating.

We spoke earlier of the latent terrorism in the rule of law, which has been seen many times in history since the Old Testament, and is often a postrevolutionary feeling. A great experience has been shared: the society feels drawn together into a single body, and social and individual standards become, for a necessarily brief period, assimilated. Plato's *Republic* outlines an ideal society on the analogy of the wise man's mind, where the reason is a dictatorial philosopher-king, the will a ruthless thought-police hunting down every subversive impulse, and the natural impulses of appetite, though allowed to function, are rigidly controlled. At the end of the ninth book Socrates suggests that such a society could perhaps never exist, but that wise men may and do exist, and the wise man would live by the laws of such a republic, whatever his actual social context. As an allegory of the wise man's mind, the *Republic* is a powerful vision; as an ideal social order, it would be a fantastic tyranny.

Similarly, the Sermon on the Mount is in part a commentary on the Ten Commandments in which the negative commands not to kill or commit adultery or steal are positively stated as an enthusiasm for human life, a habitual respect for the dignity of a woman, a delight in sharing goods with those who need them. Such a Gospel, Paul says, sets one free of the law—and of course we do not get free of the law by breaking the law, only more fouled up with it than ever. But the standards of the highly integrated individual are far more rigorous than those that apply to society in general, hence the Gospel made into a new social law would again be the most frightful tyranny. Thus, according to Milton, Jesus condemns divorce because "marriage" for him means spiritual marriage, the model of which is Adam and Eve in Eden, for each of whom there was, very exactly, no one else. Such a marriage would not be "consummated," which means finished, at the first sexual union, but only by the death of one of the partners. But to assume that every sexual liaison or marriage contract in ordinary society is a spiritual marriage of this type would pervert the Gospel into a new law.

Whether Milton is right or wrong, he is assuming a prophetic rather than a legal basis for the Gospel. Let us go back to Plato for another illustration. The one thing which has caught everyone's imagination in Plato is the figure of Socrates, the archetypal teacher and prophet, "corrupting" the youth of Athens by showing them that when they express social stereotypes about love or courage or justice or pleasure they have not the faintest idea what they are talking about. We see this Socrates, in the *Apology* and the *Phaedo*, facing martyrdom without making any concession to the ignorance and stupidity of his accusers. But Plato himself was a revolutionary thinker, and in the *Laws* he draws up a blueprint for his own post-revolutionary society. In that society all teachers are to be most strictly supervised and instructed what to teach: everything depends on their complete subservience to the overall social vision. Socrates does not appear in the *Laws*, and no such person as Socrates could exist in such a society. We should be careful to understand what Plato is doing here. He is really assuming that those who condemned Socrates were right in principle, and wrong only—if wrong at all by that time—in their application of it.

Similarly, Christianity is founded on a prophet who was put to death as a blasphemer and a social menace, hence any persecuting Christian is assuming that Pilate and Caiaphas were right in principle, and should merely have selected a different victim. The significance of the life of Jesus is often thought of as a legal significance, consisting in a life of perfect morality, or total conformity to a code of right action. But if we think of his significance as prophetic rather than legal, his real significance is that of being the one figure in history whom no organized human society could possibly put up with. The society that rejected him represented all societies: those responsible for his death were not the Romans or the Jews or whoever happened to be around at the time, but the whole of mankind down to ourselves and doubtless far beyond. "It is expedient that one man die for the people," said Caiaphas (John 18:14), and there has never been a human society that has not agreed with him.

What primarily distinguishes Christianity (and Judaism) from most Oriental religions, it seems to me, is this revolutionary and prophetic element of confrontation with society. This element gives meaning and shape to history by presenting it with a dialectical challenge. From this point of view, the root of evil in human life cannot be adequately described as ignorance, or the cure for it correctly described as enlightenment. The record of human cruelty and folly is too hideous for anything but the sense of a corrupted will to come near to a diagnosis. Hence Jesus was simply the compassionate Jesus as Buddha was the compassionate Buddha. His work, though it includes the teaching of ways of enlightenment, does not stop there, but goes through a martyrdom and a descent into death. Two implications here are of especial importance for our present purpose. One, a specifically historical situation is latent in any "enlightenment": man has to fight his way out of history and not simply awaken from it. Two, the ability to absorb a complete individual is, so far, beyond the capacity of any society, including those that call themselves Christian.

Anti-Semitism is a long-standing corruption of Christianity, and one of the more rationalized pretexts for it is the notion that the legalism condemned in the New Testatment is to be identified with Judaism. But this is a very dubious interpretation of even the most polemical parts of the New Testament, and is not found at all in the teaching of Jesus. Jesus always attacks a quite specific elite or pseudo-elite of chief priests, scribes, lawyers, Pharisees, Sadducees, and other "blind guides" (Matt. 23:24), but not the precepts of the religion he was brought up in himself. What Jesus condemned in Pharisaism is as common in Christianity as in any other religion. The attack on legalism is in a quite different context: it means accepting the standards of society, and society will always sooner or later line up with Pilate against the prophet.

In the book of Leviticus the ritual for the Day of Atonement, . . . consisted in separating a symbolic figure of a goat ("scapegoat," as the Authorized Version calls it), which represented their accumulated sin, from the community of Israel. The antitype of this, in the Christian view, is the separation of Christ from the human community, an atonement that reunites God with man. It was unfortunate for the English language that the originally comic pronunciation of "one" as "wun" should have caught on, as it obscures the connection of "one" with other words derived from it, such as "alone" and "only." More relevant for us at the moment is its obscuring of the fact that the radical meaning of "atonement" is "unifying." The Authorized Version speaks of atonement mainly in the sense of making reparation for sin, and in the Old Testament context. The "unifying" implications of atonement take us much further than this. They suggest that a channel of communication between the divine and the human is now open, and hence the whole metaphorical picture of the relation of man and God has to be reversed. Man does not stand in front of an invisible but objective power making conciliatory gestures of ritual and moral obligation to him: such gestures express nothing except his own helplessness.

Let us take an example from outside the biblical area. The Roman Saturnalia festival, in which masters waited on their slaves in memory of the golden age of Saturn, was a dumb, helpless gesture which said symbolically that the slave structure of Roman society was all wrong, but that nothing could or would be done about it. For Paul and the author of Hebrews the old sacrificial rituals, like the Saturnalia, were "vanity": empty actions in an empty world, even though the good will they expressed had a symbolic or typical value. In the changed metaphor man has an infinite energy behind him that is now available to him: a God who is invisible because he does the seeing. The metaphor of a God behind, a power that can do anything through man, seems implicit in Jesus' strong emphasis on God as a "Father," the hidden source of his own energy. Once again, changes in metaphor are fundamental changes, and here we may glimpse the possibility of getting past the pseudo-issues growing out of the metaphor of a divine presence in front of us, who may be believed or disbelieved "in" because he may or may not be "there." Theist and atheist are at one in regarding personality as the highest category known to experience. Whether it is possible for human personality to be connected with and open to a divine one that is its own infinite extension may still be a question, but the more solid the metaphorical basis for either side, the more possibility there is of mutual understanding.

So far we have spoken in individual terms, but the Gospel also brings in a new conception of "Israel" as the citizens of the kingdom of God. The notion that any group of such citizens, such as women or slaves, is inherently second-class is nonsense (Gal. 3:28). Such a society is not the ordinary society out of which we grow from birth, but a re-created society growing out of an individual. Its type is the society descended from an eponymous ancestor, as the society of Israel grew out of the body of Jacob. The conception of a possible social resurrection, a transformation that will split the world of history into a spiritual kingdom and a hell, is a part of the Gospel teaching itself, though an easy part to misunderstand. I think we do misunderstand it if we assume that everyone in the New Testament period thought that the world was coming to an end at once, and that consequently Jesus himself must have been equally confused about the matter. No doubt there were many for whom the "end of the world" was a simply future event, but we have suggested that a rather subtler notion of time than that seems to be involved in Jesus' teachings.

Women as Paradigms of True Discipleship

Elisabeth Schüssler Fiorenza

Where the post-Pauline writers seek to stabilize the socially volatile situation of coequal discipleship by insisting on patriarchal dominance and submission structures, not only for the household but also for the church, the original Gospel writers move to the other end of the social "balance" scale. They insist on altruistic behavior and service as the appropriate praxis and ethos of Christian leadership. As we have seen, egalitarian leadership, sociologically speaking, is "shifting" or "alternating" leadership. To stabilize shifting situations of alternating leadership and power, one can introduce either permanent status relationships of dominance and submission or those which call forth altruistic behavior that benefits the whole group.

Independent of each other the evangelists called Mark and John gathered traditional materials and stories about Jesus and his first followers and molded them into the gospel form. They did so not because of antiquarian or nostalgic interest in the past of Jesus' life, but because they believed that the resurrected Lord was, at that time, speaking to their communities in the words and deeds of Jesus of Nazareth. Both Gospels emphasize service and love as the core of Jesus' ministry and as the central demand of discipleship. The Gospel of Mark was written at approximately the same time as Colossians, which marks the beginnings of the patriarchal household–cold trajectory. The final redaction of the Gospel of John emerges at about the same time as the Pastorals and letters of Ignatius, and might address the same communities in Asia Minor. It is, therefore, significant that the first writers of gospels articulate a very different ethos of Christian discipleship and community than that presented by the writers of the injunctions to patriarchal submission, although both address Christian communities in the last third of the first century.

THE GOSPEL OF MARK

The unknown Christian who brought the various traditions and stories about Jesus of Nazareth together into a coherent narrative structure did so in order to strengthen the faith and praxis of the Christian community to whom s/he writes. Though scholars differ in their assessment of the theological tendencies and the historical situation in Mark, most agree that "the Jesus tradition was appropriated in this gospel in such a manner as to bear directly on the needs, responsibilities, self-understanding, anxieties, conflicts and weaknesses that characterized their community in their time" (H. C. Kee, *Community of the New Age: Studies in Mark's Gospel*). The kind of communinity to which Mark writes is mirrored in his/her picture of the disciples, their questions, reactions, and failures.

Discipleship in Mark is understood as a literal following of Jesus and of his example. Mark's christological emphasis, however, is on the necessity of Jesus' suffering, execution, and death. True understanding of Jesus messiahship does not come through the experience of miracles or through his public preaching or private instructions, but only in and through "taking up the cross" and following him on the way of suffering and death. The true meaning of Jesus is not perceived in his miracles or in his teaching with authority, then, but only in and through the experience of persecution and suffering for the Gospel's sake.

Suffering is not an end in itself, however, but is the outcome of Jesus' life-praxis of solidarity with the social and religious outcasts of his society. The threefold announcement of Jesus' suffering in 8:22–10:52 is followed each time by the misunderstanding of the disciples and Jesus' call to discipleship as a "following" on the way to the cross. Just as rejection, suffering, and execution as a criminal are the outcome of the preaching and life-praxis of Jesus, so will they be the fate of the true disciple. In Mark's view, this is the crucial christological insight that determines both Jesus' ministry and Christian discipleship. This theology of death and suffering is developed for Christians who are being persecuted, handed over to the sanhedrins, beaten in synagogues, and standing trial before kings and governors "for Jesus' sake." Such arrests and trials are occasions for "giving witness" and "preaching the gospel in the whole world," for testifying in the power of the Spirit. They are instigated by hatred for Christians, even by their closest relatives and friends: "Brother will betray brother to death, and the father his child; children will rise against their parents and have them put to death" (13:12). Thus the Markan Gospel situates the persecutions and sufferings of its community in the context of tensions within their own household. While the writers of 1 Peter or the Pastorals seek to lessen these tensions by advocating adaptation to the dominant society and avoidance of giving offense, the Markan Jesus clearly states that giving offense and experiencing suffering must not be shunned. A true disciple of Jesus must expect suffering, hatred, and persecution.

The section on "true discipleship" (8:22–10:52) is introduced and concluded with miracle stories about the healing of blind persons. The second healing story emphasizes that faith has the power to save and to enable one to walk the road of suffering discipleship. Thus the blind man who is healed and can see again becomes the paradigm of Jesus' true disciple. These two healing stories frame the three predictions of Jesus' suffering, execution, and resurrection. All three follow the same literary pattern: after the prediction is pronounced (8:31; 9:31; 10:33f.), a problem of misunderstanding occurs (8:32f.; 9:32; 10:35–41), which in turn is followed by an instruction on the nature of true discipleship (8:34–38; 9:33–37; 10:42–45).

While the first instruction on true discipleship is addressed to all the disciples, the second and third specifically address the twelve and discuss their form of leadership. Whereas the first instruction is an invitation to follow Jesus in suffering and persecutions even to the point of jeopardizing one's life, the latter two address the question of leadership in the community. Both stress that the greatest, that is, the leaders in the community, must become the least, that is, the servants of all. In the first section the paradigm for such leadership behavior is a child/slave who in antiquity was totally powerless and at the mercy of the *paterfamilias*. Unlike the post-Pauline texts which admonish slaves and children to obedience and submission, the Markan Jesus exhorts those who are first to accept fully such persons of low status and to become their servants.

However, just as the disciples—with Peter as their spokesperson—do not comprehend Jesus' announcements of the necessity of suffering and death, so they fail to understand his invitation to appropriate Christian leadership. The third call to suffering discipleship, therefore, makes the same point even more forcefully. The sons of Zebedee, James and John, ask for the places of glory and power in Jesus' empire. Jesus points out that they are not promised glory and power but suffering and persecution. He explicitly stresses that while pagan leadership is based on power and domination of others, among Christians such patriarchal relationships of domination are prohibited. The leaders of the community must be servants of all and those who are preeminent must become slaves of all.

Community leaders are not to take the position of rulers but rather that of slaves because Jesus gave his life for the liberation of many. His death is understood as a ransom, as money paid for the liberation of slaves. The text does not speak of liberation from sins but of making free citizens of many. Jesus' death—understood as the liberation of many people—prohibits any relationship of dominance and submission. Leaders and highly esteemed members of the community must become equal with the lowest and socially weakest members of the community by becoming their servants and slaves. Equality is to be achieved through altruism, through the placing of interests of others and of the community first.

Whereas post-Pauline writers advocate adaptation to their society in order to lessen tensions with that society and thus to minimize the suffering and persecution of Christians, the writer of Mark's Gospel insists on the necessity of suffering and makes it quite clear that such suffering must not be avoided, especially not by adapting the structures of Christian community and leadership to Greco-Roman structures of dominance and submission. Whereas the post-Pauline writers appropriate the power of the *paterfamilias* for the leadership of the community and appeal to Christ's example in order to advocate freely chosen submission and suffering for slaves, Mark's Gospel insists that genuine Christian leadership can only be exercised as freely chosen servanthood and slavery of those who claim greatness and precedence in the Christian community. Peter, however, together with the eleven, does not understand Jesus' teaching about his own suffering or that which characterizes true Christian leadership.

Scholars agree that Mark's portrayal of the leading male disciples is rather critical and almost negative. Not only do they misunderstand Jesus and his mission, they also misconstrue his nature and identity. Finally, they betray, deny, and abandon him during the time of his arrest and execution. Despite Jesus' special instructions and severe reprimands, they fail to comprehend both Jesus' suffering messiahship and his call to suffering discipleship. While some exegetes attempt to soften the critical features of the Markan portrayal of the leading male disciples, others suggest that this redactional criticism aims at correcting a false christology on the part of Mark's "opponents" who understand Jesus either as a great miracle worker or a political Messiah, but reject Jesus' teachings on suffering. Such a christology might have been advocated by the leadership of the church in Jerusalem, but Mark advocates for his community a different christology.

Such a characterization of Mark's "opponents" in terms of a false christology fails to account sufficiently for the fact that the three predictions of Jesus' passion are not ends in themselves but climax in the call to suffering discipleship and domination-free leadership. What is at stake is right leadership. This interpretation is supported by the whole Markan context which addresses other problems of communal life and Christian praxis. The christological statements in this section on discipleship function theologically to undergird the Markan Jesus' insistence on suffering discipleship and ministerial service. Domination-free leadership in the community and being prepared to undergo sufferings and persecutions are interconnected.

The misunderstanding and incomprehension of suffering discipleship exemplified by the twelve turns into betrayal and denial in the passion narrative. Judas betrays Jesus, Peter denies him, and all the male disciples abandon him and flee into hiding. But while the circle of the twelve male disciples does not follow Jesus on his way to the cross for fear of risking their lives, the circle of women disciples exemplifies true discipleship. Throughout the Gospel Mark distinguishes between the circle of the twelve and a wider circle of disciples who, as Jesus' "very own," have received the mystery of the "empire of God" (4:11). Though the twelve are identified as men, through the list of names taken over by Mark from tradition, the wider circle of disciples are not identified as males. That Mark's androcentric language functions as inclusive language becomes now apparent in the information that women disciples have followed Jesus from Galilee to Jerusalem, accompanied him on the way to the cross, and witnessed his death. Just as in the beginning of the Gospel Mark presents four leading male disciples who hear Jesus' call to discipleship, so at the end s/he presents four leading women disciples and mentions them by name. The four women disciples—Mary of Magdala, Mary, the daughter or wife of

James the younger, the mother of Joses, and Salome—are preeminent among the women disciples who have followed Jesus, just as Peter, Andrew, James, and John are preeminent among the twelve. Though the twelve have forsaken Jesus, betrayed and denied him, the women disciples, by contrast, are found under the cross, risking their own lives and safety. That they are well aware of the danger of being arrested and executed as followers of political insurrectionist crucified by the Romans is indicated in the remark that the women "were looking from afar." They are thus characterized as Jesus' true "relatives."

Mark uses three verbs to characterize the discipleship of the women under the cross: They *followed* him in Galilee, they *ministered* to him, and they *"came up with him* to Jerusalem" (15:41). The verb *akolouthein* characterizes the call and decision for discipleship (1:18). In 8:34 and 10:28 Jesus insists that following him meant "to take up the cross," that is, to accept the danger of being executed (8:34). In pointing out that the disciples have left everything and followed Jesus, Peter is told that their reward here is both the new familial community and persecution. The women are thus characterized as true disciples of Jesus who have left everything and have followed him on the way, even to its bitter end on the cross.

The second verb, *diakonein,* emphasizes that the women disciples have practiced the true leadership demanded of the followers of Jesus. We have seen that *diakonein* cannot be restricted to table service only, since *diakonia* summarizes the whole ministry of Jesus, who does not subordinate and enslave others in the manner of gentile rulers (10:42), but is the suffering servant who liberates and elevates them from servitude. Similarly, those who exercise leadership in the community must take the last place on the community's social scale and exercise their leadership as servitude. Like Peter's mother-in-law (1:31), the women under the cross are characterized as those disciples who have understood and practiced true Christian leadership.

The last verb, *synanabainein,* refers not only to the four leading women disciples but to all the women disciples who had followed Jesus from Galilee to Jerusalem. Interestingly enough, apart from this passage, this verb is found only in Acts 13:31 where it refers to those who had encountered the resurrected Lord and become his witnesses:

And for many days he appeared to those who came up with him from Galilee to Jerusalem, who are now his witnesses to the people.

The women who have followed Jesus from Galilee to Jerusalem are thus characterized as apostolic witnesses. Whereas Acts presents the twelve as the foremost apostolic witnesses, Mark characterizes as such the women disciples under the cross. They are also mentioned after Jesus has died and the way into the Temple sanctuary has been opened to all. Together with the Roman centurion who—as witness of the suffering and death of Jesus—confesses him as the Son of God, the women disciples under the cross signify that the community of Mark, including its leadership, was open across social, religious, sexual, and ethnic lines. This community no longer acknowledges any cultic purity laws (cf. chaps. 5 and 7) and rejects for its own leadership the dominance-submission pattern prevalent in Greco-Roman society and apparently advocated by some leading Christian authorities.

A similar indirect polemic against the male disciples is also indicated in the beginning and end of the passion narrative. It is a woman who recognizes Jesus' suffering messiahship and, in a prophetic-sign action, anoints Jesus for his burial, while "some" of the disciples reprimand her. Further, it is a servant woman who challenges Peter to act on his promise not to betray Jesus. In doing so she unmasks and exposes him for what he is, a betrayer. Finally, two women, Mary of Magdala and Mary (the mother) of Joses, witness the place where Jesus was buried (15:47), and three women receive the news of his resurrection (16:1–8). Thus at the end of Mark's Gospel the women disciples emerge as examples of suffering discipleship and true leadership. They are the apostolic eyewitnesses of Jesus' death, burial, and resurrection.

Such a positive interpretation of the emerging women disciples at the end of Mark's Gospel, however, seems prohibited by 16:8, the last verse of the Gospel. Here it seems that the evangelist introduces the women disciples in order to show that like the twelve the women disciples also failed the test of true discipleship. By adding v. 7 and 8b to a traditional resurrection account, Mark at first glance seems to expose the women as disobedient to the command of the youth or angel. Theodore Weeden has therefore concluded that the twelve never received the news about the resurrection and thus were never rehabilitated in the eyes of the Markan community. The Gospel seems to climax with the failure of the women disciples to announce the good news of the resurrection, with their disobedient flight and silent fear. If this is the case then the other disciples together with Peter and the twelve never heard the gospel of the resurrection.

However, such a reading of the Gospel's ending is not necessary. It overlooks the fact that the women disciples flee not from the angel and the resurrection news but from the tomb. While all the disciples and the unknown young man flee at the arrest of Jesus, the women flee from the tomb that is empty. To be found at the tomb of someone executed was to risk being identified as his/her follower, and possibly even being arrested. The women's fear therefore was well founded. The statement that they kept silent because of this fear of being apprehended and executed like Jesus does not imply that they did not obey the command of the angel, however. "Generalized instruction to keep silence does not prevent disclosure to a specified individual (or group). It simply relates to the 'public at large'." For instance, in Mark 1:44 Jesus charges the healed leper: "See that you say nothing to anyone; but go show yourself to the priest. . . ." The command to be silent does not exclude the information that must be given to the priest. Similarly, the silence of the women vis-à-vis the general public does not exclude fulfilling the command to "go and tell the disciples and Peter," and communicating the resurrected Lord's message of his going ahead to Galilee where they shall see him. Mark 16:7 and 8b, therefore, are not to be related as command and disobedience of the command, but as command and obedience which brings the message to special designated persons but does not inform anyone else.

Despite the extraordinary fear for their lives the women disciples stood with Jesus in his suffering, sought to honor him in his death, and now become the proclaimers of his resurrection. They preserve the messianic identity of the crucified and resurrected Lord which is entrusted to the circle of the disciples. Despite their fear and flight the good news of the resurrection is carried on. The Markan community still experiences this fear of Mary Magdalene and the other women. Like Peter, the community is tempted to betray Jesus in order to avoid suffering. The community gathers in secrecy and in house churches. It knows that the revelation of Jesus' true identity as the suffering Messiah is given to his disciples but not to outsiders. It struggles to avoid the pattern of dominance and submission that characterizes its social-cultural environment. Those who are the farthest from the center of religious and political power, the slaves, the children, the Gentiles, the women, become the paradigms of true discipleship.

THE GOSPEL OF JOHN

The Fourth Gospel is written some twenty to thirty years after Mark. Although it is an independent version of the gospel form, it also can be divided into three sections: Jesus' public ministry (the book of signs: chaps. 1–12), a special section of instructions for his disciples (chaps. 13–17), and the passion and resurrection narrative (chaps. 18–20). Chapter 21 probably was added by a final redactor. While Mark's instructions on discipleship center primarily around the necessity of suffering messiahship and suffering discipleship, the Johannine discipleship instructions focus on the motif of altruistic love and service, though this topic is also found in Mark's discipleship instructions.

Like the Markan church, the Johannine community experiences persecutions and difficulties. The "world" not only hated and killed Jesus because of the revelation he had to give, it also hates Jesus' disciples who, like him, are witnesses before the world (John 15:27; 17:14). Jesus had revealed that God loves the world (3:16)—or in the words of 1 John that God is love (4:8). Having shown his love by giving his life for his own, by making them "friends," Jesus asks them therefore to love each other. The disciples give witness to the world insofar as they love one another (13:34f.). This love is at its greatest when they give their life for their friends (15:13), for in doing so they demonstrate that they are not "of this world," that is, that their life is defined not by the destructive powers of hate and death but by the life-giving power of God revealed in Jesus. As Jesus has loved them until the last second of his life, so the disciples are to love one another. In and through their love for each other they are called to give public witness to the life-giving power of God's love revealed in Jesus. By this *praxis of agape* all people will know that they are Jesus' disciples. Thus discipleship must be lived in service and love. It must be lived as a public witness which indicts the hate and death-dealing powers of "the world." Although the Fourth Gospel is interested in a political apology vis-à-vis Roman political authorities, it does not advocate an adaptation of the community to Greco-Roman patriarchal power structures. It insists that Jesus' power and community of friends called forth by him is not "of this world" of hate and death.

That the Johannine community is an alternative community clearly comes to the fore in Jesus' sign-action, washing his disciples' feet. Whereas in the Pastorals the enrolled widows are required "to have washed the feet of the saints," in the Fourth Gospel this is Jesus' action of love to be followed by *all* his disciples. Jesus' whole ministry and his revelation of God is summed up in this scene:

> Now before the feast of the Passover, when Jesus knew that
> his hour had come to depart out of this world to the Father,

having loved his own who were in the world, he loved
them to the end. [He] rose from supper, laid aside his
garments, and girded himself with a towel. Then he poured
water into a basin, and began to wash the disciples' feet, and
to wipe them with the towel with which he was girded. . . .
When he had washed their feet and taken his garments, and
resumed his place, he said to them, "Do you know what I
have done to you? You call me teacher and Lord; and you
are right, for so I am. If then I, your Lord and teacher, have
washed your feet, you also ought to wash one another's
feet. For I have given you an example that you also should
do as I have done to you. Truly, truly I say to you, a servant
[or slave] is not greater than [his/her] master; nor is [s/he]
who is sent greater than [s/he] who sent [him/her]. If you
know these things, blessed are you if you do them.

(13:1, 4–5, 12–17)

The act of the foot washing and Jesus' interpretation of it are inter-
rupted by the misunderstanding and protest of Peter, who does not
understand that the disciples are already clean and holy through the
word that Jesus has spoken to them (15:3; 17:17). The purpose of the
symbolic sign-action is not ritual cleansing but the completion of Jesus'
relevation in his praxis of service and love. If Peter fails to receive the
service of love he has no part in Jesus and his ministry.

If relationships of equality are characterized by shifting relationships of power and by alternating leadership open to every member of
the community, then the Johannine Jesus advocates the exercise of
leadership and power through alternating service and love among the
disciples who are understood as a community of friends. Therefore,
the Fourth Gospel never stresses the special leadership of the twelve
among the disciples, even though it knows of the circle of the twelve. All
the members of the community have received the Spirit, are born
anew (3:3–9), and have received the powers of the new creation. The
resurrected Lord appears to all the disciples, not just to the twelve. All
the disciples are the recipients of the same mission Jesus had (20:21),
they all receive the Spirit (v. 22), and they are all given the power to
forgive sins (v. 23). If Raymond E. Brown is correct in his assumption
that the pre-Gospel narrative referred to the eleven, then the fourth
evangelist has changed the tradition deliberately to refer to all the
disciples and not primarily to the twelve (cf. Matt. 16:19; 18:18;

28:16–20). The Johannine community of friends understands itself primarily as a community of disciples. The Beloved Disciple is their apostolic authority and symbolic center. This community is constituted as the discipleship of equals by the love they have for one another.

The disciple whom Jesus loved is historically not identified by name. He appears for the first time at the Last Supper, characterized as the hour "when Jesus having loved his own, now showed his love for them to the very end." The Johannine Jesus celebrates his Last Supper not just with the twelve but with all the disciples. The resurrected Lord appears to all the disciples, gives them his peace and entrusts them with his mission. By enlivening them with the Spirit he constitutes all of them as the new creation (cf. Gen. 2:7) and empowers all of them to forgive sins, to bind and to loose (20:19–23). Therefore, the Johannine Jesus likens the "hour" of his exaltation on the cross and the time of the disciples' bereavement to the experience a pregnant woman has before and after giving birth. Just as the woman experiences anxiety and sorrow in anticipation of the child's birth, so the disciples are sorrowful and afraid because of Jesus' departure. But just as the woman is glad and full of joy when the child is born, so the disciples will have peace and joy after their new life and future is revealed in Jesus' resurrection (16:20–22).

Though the term *disciple* is inclusive of the twelve and though the fourth evangelist knows of their leading role in the tradition, s/he nevertheless explicitly contrasts the Beloved Disciple with Peter. The Johannine community clearly regards the twelve and their spokesman Peter as belonging to Jesus' "own," but by contrasting the community's hero with Peter they implicitly maintain the superiority of their own form of discipleship over that of Petrine Christianity. Though Peter is rehabilitated in the redactional chapter 21, the bulk of the Gospel narrative points in the other direction. Under pressure he denies that he is "a disciple of Jesus" (18:17–25); at the Last Supper Peter depends on the Beloved Disciple for information (13:23–26); he is not found under the cross of Jesus the hour when the new community is born (19:26f.); he is not the first to believe in the resurrection (20:2–10); and he does not recognize the resurrected Lord (21:7) as the Beloved Disciple does.

Thus Brown seems to be correct in his conclusion that the "Johannine Christians, represented by the Beloved Disciple, clearly regard themselves as closer to Jesus and more perceptive" than the churches who claim Peter and the twelve as their apostolic authority. One of those Christians claiming the name and authority of Peter is the writer of the first letter of Peter, who insists on the submission of slaves and wives. The dispute between Johannine and Petrine Christianity seems not to have centered on christological issues but on questions of discipleship. Chapter 21 acknowledges Peter's pastoral leadership of nurture but only on the condition that he "loves" Jesus, that is, that he subscribes to the altruistic leadership advocated by the Johannine Jesus (21:15–19).

The discipleship and leadership of the Johannine community is inclusive of women and men. Although the women mentioned in the Fourth Gospel are examples of discipleship for women as well as men, it is nevertheless astonishing that the evangelist gives women such a prominent place in the narrative. S/he begins and ends Jesus' public ministry with a story about a woman, Mary, the mother of Jesus, and Mary of Bethany. Alongside the Pharisee Nicodemus s/he places the Samaritan woman; alongside the christological confession of Peter s/he places that of Martha. Four women and the Beloved Disciple stand under the cross of Jesus. Mary of Magdala is not only the first to witness the empty tomb but also the first to receive an appearence of the resurrected Lord. Thus at crucial points of the narrative women emerge as exemplary disciples and apostolic witnesses. Although the story about the woman caught in adultery is a later addition to the Gospel's text, the interpolator nevertheless had a fine sense for the dynamics of the narrative which places women at crucial points of development and confrontation. That such a preeminence of women in the Johannine community and its apostolic tradition caused consternation among other Christians is expressed in 4:27f. where the disciples are "shocked" that Jesus converses and reveals himself to a woman. The evangelist emphasizes, however, that the male disciples knew better than to openly question and challenge Jesus' egalitarian praxis.

Jesus' public ministry begins with a miracle at a wedding in Cana. The pre-Johannine story, which might have belonged to the miracle source taken over and redacted by the evangelist, stresses Mary's influence as the mother of Jesus, since she intervenes for her friends to compel Jesus to work a miracle. The tensions in the text indicate that the evangelist has modified this traditional account by inserting v. 4: "Woman, what have you to do with me? My hour has not yet come." Since we have no precedent in Jewish or Greco-Roman sources for a son to address his mother as "woman," the address distances Jesus from his biological mother and rejects any claims she might have on him because of her family relationship to him. At the same time, it places Mary of Nazareth at the same level as the Samaritan woman (4:21) and Mary of Magdala (20:13), both of whom were apostolic witnesses and exemplary disciples. Here Mary proves herself to be such. Despite the rebuff she admonishes the servants *(diakonoi):* "Do whatever he tells you." If the Johannine community acknowledged *diakonoi* as leading ministers of the community, then Mary's injunction has symbolic overtones for the readers of the Gospel. In the beginning of the gospel ministry the leaders of the community are admonished: "Do whatever he tells you." Further, it is stressed that this exhortation must be accepted not because it comes from Jesus' mother but because it is given by a woman disciple.

The revelatory dialogue of Jesus with the Samaritan woman progresses through misunderstandings to a greater perception of the revealer. The whole section climaxes in the confession of the Samaritans that Jesus is the "savior of the world." The dramatic dialogue is probably based on a missionary tradition that ascribed a primary role to a woman missionary in the conversion of the Samaritans. Exegetes agree that the Johannine community had a strong influx of Samaritan converts who might have been catalysts for the development of the high christology of the Gospel. The present Johannine community reaps the harvest made possible by the missionary endeavors of a woman who initiated the conversion of the Samaritan segment of the community. In the "interlude" about missionary work (4:31–38) Jesus uses the Pauline verb *kopian* to describe her missionary work, "I have sent you to reap what you have not labored for. Others have labored, and you have come in to enjoy the fruits of their labor" (4:38). Since the term is used here in a technical missionary sense, the woman is characterized as the representative of the Samaritan mission.

Missionary conversion is understood by way of analogy to the call to discipleship. Just as Andrew calls his brother Peter into the discipleship of Jesus by telling him, "We have found the Messiah" (1:40–42), so the woman's testimony motivates the Samaritans to come to him (4:39). Just as Nathanael becomes a disciple because Jesus knew what he had done under the fig tree (1:46–49), so the woman becomes a witnessing disciple because "he told me all that I ever did" (4:29). In the 17:20 it is stressed that Jesus prayed not only for the disciples but also for "those who believe in him through their word." Using almost the same words, 4:39 states that many Samaritans believed in him "because of the words of the woman who testified." However, they come to full faith because of the self-revelation of Jesus. The Johannine community in Samaria no longer bases its faith on the proclamation of the missionaries but on its own experience of the presence and revelation of Jesus.

Finally, it is significant to note the response of the woman to Jesus and the content of his revelation. Faith and revelation are the two motifs that dominate the dramatic narrative. How revelation and faith interact dialectically can be seen in the progress of the christological statements: Jew (v. 9), Lord (v. 11), greater than our father Jacob (v. 12), prophet (v. 19), salvation comes from the Jews (v. 22), Messiah (v. 25), I am (v. 26), *Christos* (vv. 25, 29), Savior of the world (v. 42). In addition to the major topic of mission, two additional themes are dealt with: the gift of the revealer—living water—and the worship of the new community.

The question of the fullness of life which the revealer gives and promises is elucidated throughout the Gospel. Wine, water, bread, light, truth, way, vine, door, word, are essential to human life because without them people perish. These images not only designate Jesus himself but, at the same time, his gifts for life, the living and life-giving divine powers that lead to eternal life as well. It is the Spirit who creates and sustains such life (cf. 3:8, 6:63). The life mediated through the Spirit

> is the great gift of salvation, representing an active and vital reality in persons so that the image of the source welling up unfailingly could also be applied to it.

The second theme in the revelatory dialogue with the Samaritan woman is that of "worship in sprit and truth" (4:20–24). The central symbol of religious power for the Johannine community is no longer either the Temple in Jerusalem or the one at Gerizim. Already in 2:13–22 we learned that the risen Jesus' "body" is the place where God is to be worshiped, the true temple replacing the central Jewish Samaritan symbol of religious power. For the Johannine community the time is now, when the true worshipers will worship the Father in Spirit and truth, because God is Spirit, the life-giving power to be adored. Such worship takes place in the community of believers who are born anew in the Spirit and are called to "do the truth" (3:21). It is the worship of those who are made holy through the word and for whom social-religious distinctions between Jews and Samaritans, women and men no longer have any validity.

Jesus' public ministry climaxes in the revelation that Jesus is the resurrection and the life (11:1–54). Whereas in the original miracle source the raising of Lazarus stood at the center of the story, the evangelist has placed the dialogue and confession of Martha at the center of the whole account. Central to the dialogue with Martha is the revelatory saying of Jesus in 11:25f., "I am the resurrection and the life" as well as Martha's response in v. 27: "Yes, Lord, I believe that you are the Christ, the son of God, who is coming into the world." As the raising of a dead person the raising of Lazarus is the greatest miracle and therefore the climax of the "signs" of Jesus. However the evangelist has not placed it at the end of Jesus' public ministry and the beginning of Jesus' passion because of its miraculous character, but rather to make it clear that Jesus who will be killed is in reality "the resurrection and the life." The miracle becomes a sign pointing to the true resurrection and everlasting life: to Jesus himself. Although believers may suffer human death, they have life in an ultimate sense. In faith, human life gains a new dimension that does not know ultimate death; and this new dimension of life, eternal life, is opened up through Jesus.

Martha, Mary, and Lazarus are characterized as Jesus' friends whom he loved (11:5). They are his true disciples and he is their "teacher." Martha, after receiving the revelation and expressing her faith in Jesus' word, goes and calls Mary (11:20), just as Andrew and Philip called Peter and Nathanael. As a "beloved disciple" of Jesus she is the spokeswoman for the messianic faith of the community. She confesses, however, her messianic faith not in response to the miracle but in response to Jesus' revelation and challenge: "Do you believe this?" Her confession parallels that of Peter (6:66–71), but is a christological confession in the fuller Johannine messianic sense: Jesus is the revealer who has come down from heaven. As such it has the full sense of the Petrine confession at Caesarea Philippi in the synoptics, especially in Matthew 16:15–19. Thus Martha represents the full apostolic faith of the Johannine community, just as Peter did for the Matthean community. More importantly, her faith confession is repeated at the end of the Gospel in 20:31, where the evangelist expresses the goal of her/his writing of the Gospel: "But these are written that you may believe that Jesus is the Christ, the Son of God, and that believing you may have life in his name." If Robert Fortna is correct that this summary statement concluded the signs source, then it might be possible to conjecture that the evangelist deliberately put these words of his/her source into the mouth of Martha as the climactic faith confession of a "beloved disciple" in order to identify her with the writer of the book. Such a suggestion is not inconceivable since we do not know who the writer of the Gospel was. On the other hand, such a conjecture can neither be proven nor disproven historically.

While Martha of Bethany is responsible for the primary articulation of the community's christological faith, Mary of Bethany articulates the right praxis of discipleship. She is explicitly characterized as a beloved disciple whom the teacher has specifically called. She had many followers among "the Jews" who came to believe in Jesus (11:45). Though in 11:1–54 Mary plays a subordinate role to that of Martha, in 12:1–8 she is the center of action. The evangelist might have used a tradition which was similar to Luke 10:38–42, in addition to the Markan (Matthean) anointing story of the Lukan story of a great sinner who washed Jesus' feet with her tears and dried them with her hair. The meal is in Bethany. (In Mark it is at the house of Simon the Leper, whereas here no name of the host is given). That Martha served at table could be an allusion to Luke 10:40, but it is here seen much more positively. If Corell's suggestion is right that the only established office in the Johannine community was that of *diakonos,* then Martha is characterized here as fulfilling such a ministry. In John, Mary and Martha are not seen in competition with each other, as is the case in Luke. They are characterized as the two ministers at a supper, which takes place on a Sunday evening, the day on which the early church celebrated the Eucharist.

Mary's anointing of Jesus' feet resembles the anointing story of the synoptics, but in the Johannine tradition the woman is not left unnamed. However, the feature of her wiping away the anointment with her hair is awkward and draws our attention to it. Therefore, it is possible that this gesture points forward to the Last Supper of Jesus, where Jesus washes the disciples' feet and dries them with a towel. Moreover, the centrality of Judas both in this scene and in the foot washing scene emphasizes an evangelistic intention to portray the true disciple Mary of Bethany as counterpart to the unfaithful disciple Judas Iscariot. Whereas according to Mark 14:4 "some" and according to Matthew 26:8 "the disciples" object to the waste of precious oil, in John it is Judas who objects and he does so because of avarice. Thus not only the person of Judas but also the male objection to Mary's ministry of anointing is discredited. This is also emphasized by the harsh rebuke of Jesus: "Let her alone." If we take all these different aspects of the story into account, it is most likely that the envangelist is interested in portraying Mary of Bethany as the true disciple and minister in contrast to the betrayer who was one of the twelve. She anticipates Jesus' command to wash the feet of each other as a sign for the agape praxis of true discipleship. Both stories—the messianic confession of Martha and the anointing of Jesus' feet by Mary—point to the death and resurrection of Jesus, to his hour of glorification.

According to the Fourth Gospel, women—Jesus' mother, his mother's sister, Mary, the wife of Cleopas, and Mary Magdalene—and one male disciple stood by the cross of Jesus (19:25–27). Numerous studies of this scene have been written and a variety of symbolic meanings has been suggested. The most likely meaning of the scene is probably indicated by the explicit statement that the mother of Jesus became a part of the Johannine community after the death and resurrection of Jesus. Interestingly enough, neither she nor the Beloved Disciple are mentioned by name. Here, as in chapter 2, she is addressed by the title "woman" and thus characterized as one of the apostolic women disciples. The scene then probably has a meaning similar to that of Mark 3:31–35, where the discipleship community of Jesus as the replacement for all ties and claims of the patriarchal family is also stressed. In Jesus' death the "new family" of disciples is constituted, thus making them brothers and sisters. The scene then seeks to communicate the same message given in the prologue: "He came to his own, and his own people received him not. But to all who received him, who believed in his name, he gave power to become children of God (John 1:11–12). The Beloved Disciple, then, represents the disciples of Jesus who, having left everything, now receive a "new familial community," houses, and brothers, and, sisters, and mothers, and children, and lands, and in the age to come "eternal life" (cf. Mark 10:29–30). The Johannine community seems to have an understanding similar to that of Mark, namely, that the "new familial community" will include "mothers" as well as brothers and sisters, but not fathers—because their father is God alone.

Finally, the scene might also contain some historical overtones. Though Jesus' mother is explicitly acknowledged as one of Jesus' "own" who are represented by the Beloved Disciple, Jesus' brothers are not so rehabilitated. Raymond Brown has suggested that the brothers of Jesus in the Gospel might represent Jewish Christians of inadequate faith (John 7:1–10). According to early Christian tradition James, the brother of the Lord, had received a resurrection appearance (1 Cor. 15:7), had served as leader of the Jerusalem church (cf. Gal. 1:19; 2:9; Acts 15; 21:18), and had died as a martyr in the early 60s:

This fits into the present discussion when it is remembered that James, the brother of the Lord, was followed during his life-time by a number of Jewish Christians in Jerusalem who were more conservative than Peter and Paul (Gal 2:12), and after his death he became the hero par excellence for the Jewish Christians of the second century who gradually separated from the "Great Church."

If Brown's suggestion has some historical plausibility, then it must be pointed out that the fourth evangelist distinguishes between the male and female members of Jesus' family and therefore implicitly also between male and female Jewish Christians. Not only the mother of Jesus but also her sister are among the faithful followers of Jesus. Could it be possible that women members of the Jerusalem church were more open to Johannine Christianity, thus prompting the evangelist to insist that they have become a part of the community of the Beloved Disciple?

The last woman to appear in the Fourth Gospel is Mary Magdalene who was also mentioned as standing under the cross of Jesus. She not only discovers the empty tomb but is also the first to receive a resurrection appearance. Thus in a double sense she becomes the *apostola apostolorum*, the apostle of the apostles. She calls Peter and the Beloved Disciple to the empty tomb and she is sent to the "new family" of Jesus to tell them that Jesus is ascending "to my Father and your Father, to my God and your God." In contrast to Mark 16:8 we are unambiguously told that Mary Magdalene went to the disciples and announced to them: "I have seen the Lord." She communicated the message to them which he had given to her. Thus she is the primary apostolic witness to the resurrection. Whereas Matthew, John, and the Markan appendix credit primacy of apostolic witness to Mary Magdalene, the Jewish Christian pre-Pauline confession in 1 Corinthians 15:3–6 and Luke claim that the resurrected Lord appeared first to Peter. Since the tradition of Mary Magdalene's primacy in apostolic witness challenged the Petrine tradition, it is remarkable that it has survived in two independent streams of the Gospel tradition. Moreover, later apocryphal writings—as we have seen—reflect the theological debate over the apostolic primacy of Mary Magdalene and Peter explicitly.

The story "in the garden" must not be psychologized. Mary is characterized not so much as the "great lover" of Jesus who is upset about his death for personal reasons, but rather as representative of the disciples' situation after the departure of Jesus. Her great sorrow is turned into joy as Jesus had promised in the farewell discourse. She is characterized as a faithful disciple in a threefold way.

First, Jesus addresses her as "woman" and asks: "Whom do you seek?" The Greek verb *zētein* has a rich meaning for the Johannine community which probably knew its technical meaning of "to study" and "to engage in the activities of a disciple." According to Culpepper John 13:33–35 implies

> that even though the disciples could not "seek" Jesus success-
> fully before the resurrection, subsequently (in the Johannine
> school), by observing the new commandment and remem-
> bering the words of Jesus (15:20; 16:4), they were distin-
> guished from the Jews and able to seek (and find) Jesus (the
> Word.)

Mary Magdalene is the disciple who, despite her sorrow, "seeks" Jesus and finds him.

Second, she recognizes Jesus at the moment when he calls her by name. In John 10, the discourse on the Good Shepherd, Jesus asserts: "I am the good shepherd; I know my own and my own know me" (10:14). The Good Shepherd "calls his own sheep by name and leads them out. When he has brought out all his own, he goes before them and the sheep follow him for they know his voice" (10:3–4). Just as the good shepherd lays down his life for his sheep, so Jesus loved his "own" to the end (13:1). Mary Magdalene is characterized as one of "his own" because Jesus calls her by name and she recognizes his voice.

Third, her response is that of the true disciple. She recognizes the resurrected Jesus as "teacher." As the faithful disciple who "seeks" the Lord-Sophia, Mary of Magdala becomes the primary apostolic witness to the resurrection. Like Mary of Nazareth, the nameless Samaritan woman, Martha, and Mary of Bethany (and perhaps the nameless adulteress who was not judged but saved by Jesus), she belongs to Jesus' very own disciples. Thus for the evangelist—who might have been a woman—these five women disciples are paradigms of women's apostolic discipleship as well as their leadership in the Johannine communities. As such they are not just paradigms of faithful discipleship to be imitated by women but by all those who belong to Jesus' "very own" familial community.

John Come Lately: The Belated Evangelist

Donald Foster

The writer of the Gospel of John (whom I'll simply call "John") is disquieted by his belatedness, by the fact that he comes after Matthew, Mark, and Luke (to say nothing of Q), yet wishes to write an authoritative account of Jesus' life. His motto is the Lord's motto: "I am the door of the sheep. All who came before me were thieves and robbers" (10:8). There were, of course, many before John, as before Luke, who undertook "to compile a narrative" of Jesus' life (Luke 1:1); but none of them, if we may believe John, succeeded. As we shall see, John's purpose is not to add one more to a growing heap of apocryphal gospels, nor even to write a supplement to the synoptics, but rather to provide the world—for the first time, if belatedly—with the true Gospel of Jesus Christ. John wishes to clarify the message of a badly misunderstood Son of God. And in the process, he does more than a little campaigning on his own behalf as belated evangelist.

From prologue to benediction, John's preoccupation with his late arrival to the evangelistic field has a profound effect on the shape of his narrative, for Jesus is presented throughout as the one who came late and yet remained prior in time, place, and truth. First comes the problem of the Baptist's priority. In his own lifetime, the Baptist had a much greater following than Jesus; but we read in John's Gospel that his sole purpose was to bear witness to his successor. "This was he," confesses John, "of whom I said, 'He who comes after me is *before*

From *The Bible and Narrative Tradition,* edited by Frank McConnell. © 1986 by Oxford University Press.

me' "—(*emprosthen*, prior in both time and place)—" 'for he was [and always has been] *before* me' " (*prōtos*, again, prior in both time and place, emphatically so); and it is worth noting that John's tribute is repeated fifteen verses later, but with their first "was" (*ēn*) transformed to an "is" (*estin*), thus illustrating the evangelist's point that Jesus as Logos is the preexistent victor over the "it was" of time (1:15, 30). Only the Father and the Son can say, "*I am.*" John, when asked if he is the Christ or Elijah, or "the prophet" expected to precede the Christ, must confess, "I am not" (1:21). The Baptist, unlike Christ, is not eternally present. His disciples are required rather to turn and *follow* the shepherding Lamb of God (1:29–40).

This theme is continued in John's typically allegorical fashion in his account of the wedding feast at Cana. The old wine (the word of the prophets) gives out, followed by the water (the Baptist's ministry) which fills the stone jars (even as the Baptist completed the old dispensation of the Law). Jesus then turns the water into new wine by the transforming power of the word. Much is made of the fact that the Lord's wine came last and yet is better than all that preceded it: "Every man sets forth the good wine first, and the worse when they are become drunk. You have kept the good wine until now" (2:10). Nevertheless, his mother Mary (like Israel) must be rebuked for urging him to act before the appointed hour.

When Jesus arrives in Sychar and sits beside the well of Jacob, it is already midday. In John's trope for Israel and the prophets, Jesus greets there a Samaritan who has had five men, the most recent of whom belongs to another woman. Jesus, the spiritual bridegroom, comes to her at the sixth hour, and after she has provided him with water, reveals to her the true worship of God, worship "in spirit and in truth." The woman then asks, "Are you superior to Jacob our father, who gave us the well, and drank from it himself, and his sons, and his cattle?" (4:12). The answer, of course, is yes—and the water which Jesus belatedly brings will not be drunk by *cattle*. "I know," says the woman, "that the Messiah is coming (he who is called Christ); when he comes, he will declare to us all things." Answers Jesus, *egō eimi*—"I am he," or (more literally), "*I am*" (4:25–26).

Some days later, in the evening hours, Jesus' disciples depart before him across the lake. Darkness settles over the land, but Jesus does not come. The sea rises, as a great tempest begins to blow. Still he does not come. When at last he appears, he comes to them walking on the waves, saying, *egō eimi*—"It is I," or "*I am*" (6:20). And despite his belated appearance, Jesus proves that he has full command over the arrival of his antecedents; they arrive at their destination only with his miraculous, if belated, assistance.

His brothers precede him to the autumnal Feast of Tabernacles. All the Jews then look for him, saying, "Where is he?" (7:11), but Jesus' predecessors are no help in finding him. When at last he arrives, with the feast half-over, the people marvel that he knows the Law without having had to be taught by another. "You will seek me," he tells the Jews, "and you will not find me: you cannot come where *I am*" (7:34). Then, "on the *last* day of the feast, the *great* day, Jesus stood up and cried out, saying, 'if anyone thirst, let him come to me, and drink' " (7:37).

At still another feast, again on the last day of the week, Jesus comes to the five crowded porticoes of the Pool of Bethzatha where there lies "a multitude of weak, blind, crippled, withered," and other unfortunates, patiently waiting for the angel of God—for once a year or so, an apparently whimsical angel would stir the water, and watch as the cripples and blindmen made a mad scramble for the pool; he then healed the first one in. Jesus, in surveying this woeful sight, finds there a man who has been lying at the poolside for thirty-eight years. Jesus asks him if he would like to be made whole. "Lord," the invalid replies, "I haven't a man to put me into the pool when the water is disturbed—and while I am coming, *another gets in before me*" (5:7). The poor fellow, needless to say, has an intense awareness of his inability to come first. But Jesus redeems him, saying, "Rise, take up your pallet, and walk" (5:8). Moreover, unlike the earlier incidents, water (i.e., the Baptist's ministry) is no longer a prerequisite for Jesus to perform his marvels—thereby illustrating John's words that "he must increase, but I must decrease" (3:30).

Once again in chapter nine—on the last day of the week as the night is approaching—Jesus heals a man, this time one who has been blind from the beginning, that is, from birth. The man's childhood prayers are answered at last when Jesus appears as the Logos which lightens the darkness, anointing his eyes with clay even as the Logos once fashioned father Adam out of clay. He then *sends* the man to wash in the Pool of Siloam, another figure for baptism. The order is chronologically reversed: one comes to the light through the word; baptism follows as the external sign of an inward grace already applied. And "the Jews hounded Jesus because he did such things *on the seventh day*" (5:16).

When Lazarus is ill, the Lord again arrives late. "When Jesus came, he found that Lazarus had already been in the tomb four days" (11:17). First Martha, then Mary, gently upbraids him for not having come sooner. "Lord," they tell him, "if you had been here, my brother would not have died"—but by this time, to quote the Authorized Version, "he stinketh" (11:21, 32, 39). No matter. Jesus proves his transcendence over time and time's laws by raising his friend from the dead, with the result that a great multitude of people become his followers. The Pharisees, meanwhile, with a touch of unwitting irony, turn to one another and sigh, "You see that it's no use. Look, the world is coming *after* him"—*ho kosmos opisō autou apēlthen anōthen* (12:19).

The Jews, however, refuse to come after him. As noted by C. K. Barrett and others, John always makes a distinction between the "crowd," some of whom, at least, are willing to follow Jesus, and the "Jews," who continually resist him, supposing that their fathers Abraham, Jacob, and Moses, having come first, are greater than he. These Jewish pretensions to a prior sonship are emblematized by various individuals: for example, Nicodemus ("victor over the people") cannot at first comprehend the concept of being "born from above" or "born from before" (Gk. *anōthen*). He does not perceive that Jesus, who comes *from above*, is able to beget sons *from above*, without relying on the prior seed of Abraham and Moses (3:3, 7, 31). Judas ("Judah") and Barabbas ("son of the father") are likewise Jews and would-be sons. Neither name originated with John, but he fits them neatly into his scheme of things by adding that Judas was a *thief*, not just a traitor, and Barabbas was not an insurrectionist as in the synoptics, but a *robber* (12:6; 18:40). Both men are thus identified as a figure for the Jews, those stubborn people who presume to have come before the Son. Judas and Barabbas are two of a kind: like all Jews in John's book, they are "sons of [their] father the devil."

Refusing to acknowledge the absolute preeminence of Jesus, the Jews are offended by the Lord's "I am" and outraged when he produces "signs" on the seventh day, when no work is to be done. They have no room in their hearts for a belated Son of God, for the "truth" is something revealed a long time ago to their fathers, to Abraham, Moses, and the prophets. But while the Jews continually look to supposed authorities whose hour came—and went—in ages past, Jesus stresses that his "hour has not yet come." This does not mean that he is less than Moses or Abraham—for where the Jews have been, he preceded them, and where he goes, they cannot follow—but he is, nevertheless, not to be fully manifested until the hour is late (2:4; 7:30; 8:20). It is not until the *Greeks* begin to seek him that he finally says, "Now is the hour come for the Son of Man to be glorified. . . . If anyone serves me, he must *follow* me" (12:23–26). And a voice from above confirms it.

In Gethsemane, when the Jews come to arrest Jesus, with the thief Judas leading the way, the Lord stops them with two words: *egō eimi*—"I am" (not, as in most English versions, "I am he," though again, it includes that meaning). Jesus is eternally present. The first time he tried out his "I am" on the Jews ("Before Abraham was, *I am*"), they took up stones to stone him (8:58–59). But this time, literally translated, they "went away *into the after* and fell on the earth" (*apēlthen eis ta opisō; opisō*, like *emprosthen*, is both temporal and spatial, denoting the *place of the follower* and the *time not yet arrived*—18:6). One thing that these thieves and robbers will not be able to take from Jesus is his everlasting preeminence.

But given all this, how does *Jesus'* victory over belatedness in any way solve *John's* problem? For John, too, arrives belatedly, following in the tracks of Q, Mark, Luke, Matthew, and a score of others. The answer is that John presents Jesus as the only begotten, if belated, Son of the Father, and himself in turn as the only true son of the Son. Adoptive sonship is open to everyone (1:12–13); but John's glory, like that of the Logos, is "glory as of the only begotten of the Father, full of grace and truth" (1:14). At the Last Supper, for example, only one apostle lies in the bosom of the Son (13:23), even as the Son is the only one ever to lie in the bosom of the Father (1:18). Again at the crucifixion, only one disciple is honored as spiritual son: "When Jesus saw [his] mother and [the] disciple whom he loved standing near, he said to the mother, 'Woman, behold your son!' Then said he to the disciple, 'Behold, your mother!' And from that hour the disciple took her unto his own" (19:26–27).

But may we, then, safely identify John the evangelist as "the disciple whom Jesus loved"? The answer is both yes and no, for John's Gospel is mediated by still another father, that is, John the apostle, the disciple with whom "the Johannine" school or cult identified itself. Throughout John's Gospel, there moves a mysterious figure without a name who is always at the center of the action. He is denoted always by a circumlocutionary phrase, and he stands for Johannine, as opposed to Petrine, Christianity. For example, after Jesus' arrest, it is this nameless Johannine apostle, not Simon Peter as in the synoptics, who follows Jesus into the courtyard of the High Priest. Peter follows at a safe distance and remains outside until the nameless disciple comes to the door and lets him in—for *he* is now the door of the sheep in Jesus' stead. But Peter's belated arrival proves a disaster. When he finally enters in, he betrays Jesus with his words, saying, "I am not" (18:17ff.). He means, in each instance, "I am not Jesus' disciple," but his words stand in deliberate contrast with the "I am" of Jesus (and of John). The implication is that Peter and Petrine Christianity are not eternally present, but are negated by time.

After the resurrection, these two disciples are contrasted again. The Johannine disciple runs ahead and comes to the tomb, but waits discreetly outside. "Then Simon Peter came, following him, and entered into the tomb"—but he fails to understand. When the Johannine disciple enters, he sees, and believes (20:3–8). The two disciples then go their separate ways, each to his own home (20:10). There is a nice symmetry in these two stories: while Jesus was yet on earth, it was the representative of Johannine Christianity who was closest to him, with Peter as a confused and unreliable follower. After Jesus returned to the higher world, Peter was the first to enter the place where the Son had been, and John followed. Even then, John, the faster runner, could easily have preempted him, but it was foreordained that the latter should enter in first and misconceive the truth, that the truth might be revealed instead to John, when his hour was come. Jesus once warned Peter that this would be so, though his words have not often been fully understood: "Where I am going," said the Lord to Simon, "you cannot follow me now; but you shall follow me *at the last*" (Gk. *husteron*—13:36), that is, after John shows him the way.

John undercuts Peter in other ways: Contrary to the synoptics, we read here that it was Andrew and *the Johannine disciple,* not Andrew and Peter, who were the first to follow Jesus. Peter came in third. And when Simon at last appears, Jesus calls him "*Kēphas,*" John's transliteration of the Aramaic, which, as he explains, means *Petros,* or "rock," but which to a Greek reader would have looked like *Kēphēn,* a "drone," "literary plagiarist," or "worn-out, decrepit person." Matthew, Mark, and Luke generously omit the transliteration. Moreover, the evangelist moves Peter's home from Capernaum to Bethsaida, on the far side of the lake from the village identified with Jesus, while moving the home of the Johannine apostle to Jerusalem, the city of God and of the glorified Christ. No longer is Peter the foundation of the Church, with the keys to heaven and hell in his right hand. He is instead a rather thick-headed Jew who sees the Son without perceiving, hears the message but does not understand. John likens him to those faithless Jews who asked scornfully of Jesus, "Where is this fellow ready to go that we shall not find him? Is he ready to go to the Greek dispersion and teach the *Greeks*? What is this logos which he speaks?" (7:35–36; cf. 8:36–37).

Simon Peter and Jesus do not seem to speak the same language. In John's version of the Last Supper, for example, the Lord's sacrament of footwashing utterly bewilders him; and when he wishes to know which disciple is the traitor, Peter cannot ask Jesus himself, but must defer to the Lord's beloved. If Peter is to know the truth, it must be mediated by John. Again, in John's account of Gethsemane, it is Simon Peter, and not just "one of those who stood by" (Mark 14:47), who misunderstands, draws his sword, and strikes off a man's ear. John gives the victim a name—Malchus, from the Aramaic for "king." Peter, in resisting the Lord's Passion, has rashly injured a symbolic substitute for the Lord himself, who is, paradoxically, both king and slave of the High Priest.

John undermines Peter even in his nomenclature: John prefers to call him *Simon* Peter, and stresses that he is *the son of Jonah*, Jonah being the prophet described always in early Christian literature as the one who sinfully resisted God's will in bringing the true religion to the Gentiles; and "son of" always implies in John, as in Hebrew scripture, a likeness, a following-in-the-footsteps-of. Peter is like Jonah in perceiving Christianity as a religion of and for the Jews. And John gives a patronym to Judas Iscariot. He is now Judas Iscariot, *the son of Simon*. Except in Gethsemane, John never mentions Judas without calling him the son of Simon. This does not mean that John wants us to think of Judas as the biological son of Simon, but he is certainly driving home the likeness of the two disciples who betrayed the Logos, the Son of God, with false words.

It may seem odd at first that the Johannine disciple should go nameless while these other men's names receive such detailed attention— but in order for John the evangelist to take his place as the true son, *the name of the intervening father must be effaced*. The name "John" is used here only in reference to John the Baptist—who in turn is never called "John the Baptist," or "the Baptist," but simply "John." In his typically symbolic fashion, John thus takes from the beloved apostle his birthright as the spiritual son, effacing the name of that apostle so that he, John, may assume his rightful place as the disciple whom Jesus loved, tracing his genealogy directly from Father, to Son, to himself as belated evangelist. John's relation to the son of Zebedee is precisely that of Jesus to the Baptist: one is the true son, the only begotten of the father, while the other is a mere herald, who bears witness to the light but is not that light. We may therefore hear, in chapter 5, for example, the two sons, Jesus and John, speaking in unison:

> You sent to John [the Baptist and the Apostle], and he has born witness to the truth. Not that the testimony which I receive is from man; but I say these things that you may be saved. That man was a burning and visible lamp, and for a season you were willing to rejoice in his light. But the testimony which I have is superior to that of John, for the works which my Father has granted me to make complete, these very works which I produce, bear me witness that the Father has sent me. And the Father who sent me has himself borne witness to me.
>
> (5:33–37)

John the apostle, like John the Baptist, is unworthy even to loosen the sandal-thong of the one coming after him, for "John produced no sign" (or, "no written proof," Gk. *sēmeion*—10:41). It is a commonplace of criticism to note that Jesus and John speak so much alike that it is impossible to tell where each speaker begins and ends. No two versions have the quotation marks in the same places; the above is one of many passages in which the speaker is not just Jesus or John, but both at once; here, as so often, John finds his words freighted with a double burden of truth.

The evangelist intuits that he is skating on thin ice in suggesting that his testimony is superior to that of his mentor, John the apostle, for if the Gospel was not actually dictated to him by an eyewitness, what authority does it have? John insists, therefore, that his Gospel is based on the apostle's firsthand experience—"He who saw it has borne witness; his testimony is true, and he knows that he speaks truly, that you also may believe" (19:35)—but in his narrative John goes far beyond anything the apostle could have told him, and he frequently contradicts the synoptics. How, then, can anyone be sure that his Gospel is true? This problem of authority is the same one faced by the belated Son of man, who says, "If I bear witness to myself, then my testimony is not true. There is another [John] who bears witness to me" (5:31–32); later, though, when the Jews seem to trap him, saying, Aha! here you are, bearing witness to yourself, he replies, "Well, even if I *do* bear witness to myself, my testimony is true, for I know whence I have come. . . . I bear witness to myself, and the Father who sent me bears witness to me" (8:13–18).

That John bears witness to himself is evident: he refuses to name the apostle John as his authority, and boldly contradicts all other known accounts of Jesus' life. That the Father *also* bears witness to him is something that we must take on faith. John shrewdly places the burden of proof, not on himself as narrator, but on the reader as believer. It is not enough to believe in Jesus; one must believe in the *word* of Jesus, and not in any word, but in *John's* word.

> You do not have his word [or, "the word of him"—*ton logon autou*] abiding in you, for you do not believe him whom he has sent. You search the scriptures [or, "the writings"], because you think that in them you have everlasting life, and it is they that bear witness to me, and yet you do not want to come to me that you may have life. I do not receive glory [or "opinion"—Gr. *doxa*] from men; rather, I know that you have not the love of God within you: I have come in the name of the Father, and you do not receive me; if another comes in his own name, him you will receive.
>
> (5:38–43)

Once again, we may hear Jesus and John speaking in unison. John's Logos is the way, the truth, and the life—and he who "climbs in by another way, that man is a thief and a robber" (10:1).

Unlike Matthew, Mark, and Luke, the Gospel of John is conceived "in spirit and in truth." Like the Logos of God, John's word, which seems to come last, has actually existed since the beginning; like the bread of life, it has come down "from above"; like Jesus' inner robe, his Gospel is "woven throughout from above" (Gk *anōthen*). His Gospel is prior to all. And herein lies John's superiority to those thieves and robbers who came before: their Gospels were of the letter, whereas his is pneumatic, that is, allegorical and spiritual. That John's Gospel is less literal than the synoptics is hardly a fresh observation. It is everywhere said, except by Protestant fundamentalists, that John's Gospel is insistently allegorical and that he shows a casual disregard for historical accuracy. But such statements distort John's design as much as the fundamentalist's refusal to see either the allegory or the contradictions. John is not a blind follower of Philo, or of the epistler of Hebrews. His is allegory with a difference; John's is allegorized narrative which the writer himself takes for the literal historical truth. John trusts that if all were known, he'd be proved right in every detail—he feels it in his bones. Word by word, the Logos has been revealed to him by the indwelling Father and Son. There is no point in trying to go back and check him against some hypothetical or poorly remembered historical "fact." John's word perfectly recovers the "what was" of time. Where Matthew, Mark, and Luke contradict him, they are simply wrong; and if we need proof, we need only look at how clearly the deeds of Jesus' life, as related by John, figure forth doctrinal truths in a way that the synoptic accounts can never hope to match. The implicit allegory is the *guarantee* of his narrative's historical accuracy. This is not to say that the synoptic Gospels are worthless, but only that they have been superseded (and preceded) by the eternally present Logos of John. John's relationship to Mark, for example, is that of Jesus to Moses: "If you do not believe his (literal) *grammasin,* how will you believe my (spiritual) *rēmasin?*" (5:47).

Jesus' sheep hear his voice, and they follow him. John's anxiety is that he will *not* be followed, only preceded, that his pneumatic Gospel will be rejected for the literal, thing-centered Gospels which came before. It is interesting to note that in John, whenever Jesus speaks an allegory, God's chosen people take up stones to stone him, as if to confound his allegory with a supremely literal object. John, too, must fear the stones of the literally minded. Nevertheless, John is not writing fiction. He never thinks of his Gospel as mere parable, as a narrative written to *illustrate* the truth. John, in fact, scorns parable, as does the Jesus of John's Gospel. The synoptics are the storytellers. John has nothing to tell but the truth itself—and he underscores the point with his revision of the Lazarus story: John breathes into Luke's Lazarus the breath of life, transforms him, fashions a dead parchment into a living soul. Next his "real" Lazarus is brought to life by Jesus, as Luke's was not. "Unbind him," says Jesus, "and let him go" (11:44). Nor was John's Lazarus ever "in the bosom" of father Abraham (Luke 16:22ff.), for "no man has gone up to heaven except he who came down from heaven, that is, the Son of man" (John 3:13). Moreover, Luke's father Abraham is wrong in assuming that "if they do not hear Moses and the prophets, neither will they be convinced if someone should rise from the dead" (Luke 16:31), for John not only resurrects

Lazarus, but reports that "on account of him many of the Jews went along and believed in Jesus" (12:10–11)—and the published report of Lazarus' resurrection, says John, caused a second crowd to believe, larger than the first (12:17–18). But the disparity between the two Lazarus stories of Luke and John does not mean that John's is a fiction. Quite the reverse: Jesus really *did* raise Lazarus from the dead, but Luke turned the miracle into a pathetic fiction, a "parable," to illustrate a supposed truth. John thereby turns the narrative tables upon his predecessor. In a similar vein, the Jews' false rhetorical ploy of the woman with seven husbands becomes in John's hands a real woman (about whom more later) who in turn stands as a figure for the Jews themselves.

John everywhere is at pains to tell the *true* history of Jesus' life, as opposed to the stories and rumors circulated by his forebears. For example, in the Petrine Gospel of Mark, when Jesus' "soul is anguished, even to death," he prays to the Father, saying, "All things are possible for you. Remove this cup from me" (Mark 14:34, 36). Though the Son does submit, there is a conflict between his will and that of the Father: "Yet it is *not* what *I*, but what *you*, desire" (14:36). John's Jesus is far more resolute: "Now is my soul troubled. And what shall I say? 'Father, save me from this hour'? No! it is for this very purpose that I have come to this hour!" (John 12:27). John deplores Mark's slander on the Son. Jesus must therefore turn directly to Peter in the Garden and rebuke him, saying, "Shall I not drink the cup which the Father has given me?" (18:11). He shall, and without complaining.

There are other differences. Jesus here does not preach repentance, prophesy of the end times, or debate with Jewish leaders concerning death, divorce, taxes, prayer, sabbath-keeping, burnt offerings, and charitable giving. More importantly, he is not evasive when asked whence his authority derives. The verbal sparring is for Matthew, Mark, and Luke; John's Jesus says plainly that his authority is from the Father. Nor does he refuse to give the Jews a sign. In the synoptics, "signs" (Gk. *sēmeia*) are given only by "false Christs and false prophets" and by Judas, "the betrayer" (e.g., Matt. 24:24; 26:48). Jesus there refuses to give any sign save the *sēmeion* of Jonah. In John, on the other hand, "signs" are Jesus' hallmark. He performs so many that the world itself can not contain them, and on account of his signs there are many who believe, and follow.

John's Jesus is in every way less *Jewish*. He does not exorcise demons (a Jewish custom), nor does he call the Jews his "children," and the Gentiles, "dogs." He, in turn, is never called "Rabbi" except by those who fail fully to understand the truth. And here, despite the assertions of Matthew and Luke to the contrary, the Law of Moses is strictly for the Jews and has no authority over the followers of Christ (John 8:17; 10:34; 15:25; 19:7; cf. Matt. 5:17–20). Only the Pharisees assume that those who do not know the Law are accursed (John 7:49). Here, the only requirement for eternal life is to believe in him who is sent by the Father (John 6:28–29; cf. Luke 10:25–28). Nor does Jesus have time for Jewish customs like fasting. Three days after his baptism, while Mark's Jesus is still with wild beasts in the wilderness, fasting and being tempted of Satan, John's Jesus is attending a wedding feast in the village of Cana. If he believes in fasting, he never so much as mentions it; and when, on the other hand, he goes to a Jewish festival such as the Passover or the Feast of Tabernacles, he goes not as a participant, as in the synoptics, but as a missionary. Again, in the Gospels of Matthew, Mark, and Luke, Jesus in every city enters the synagogue to teach. In the narrative portion of John's Gospel, Jesus enters a synagogue only once, to deliver his sermon on the Eucharist ("Unless you eat the flesh of the Son of man and drink his blood, you have no life in you."); and he delivers this sermon in a synagogue because the Eucharist, with its imagery of blood sacrifice, is for John an all-too-Jewish metaphor, the very un-Jewish notion of drinking blood notwithstanding (6:25–59).

In John's account of the Last Supper, the Eucharist is conspicuous by its absence. John wills to abolish the sacrament of the bread and wine, which was based on a prior Jewish feast, and to supplant it with a new, more specifically Christian sacrament, based on the doctrine that the last shall be first. He makes a concerted effort to displace the largely Jewish rites of Petrine Christianity: Jesus, after first instituting John's belated sacrament of footwashing, specifically commands his followers to "do as I have done unto you" (13:15). If the larger Christian community never took to washing one another's feet as enthusiastically as they took to the bread and wine, it is probably not John's fault. Moreover, in the synoptics, the Last Supper is *itself* a Passover meal (Mark 14:12ff; and parallels) while in John the supper comes "*before the feast of the Passover, when Jesus knew that his hour had come*" (13:1); the Passover is to be eaten instead on the following day (18:28; 19:14). John thus obliterated the temporal distinction between the Passover and the Passion, so that the Jewish rite does not come first. Jesus is then killed even as the paschal lambs are being slaughtered, as a reminder that the sacrificial lamb of the Old Testament does not come before Christ, or even "prefigure" Christ, but is a dim shadow of the eternally present Christ. It is not even a very adequate metaphor: the only one ever to call Jesus the sacrificial "Lamb of God" is his Jewish predecessor (1:29, 36). A lamb is a follower. The Son follows no one, least of all the fathers of the Jews.

Now if, as we have seen, the evangelist feels ambivalent toward the son of Zebedee as his spiritual forebear, and toward Matthew, Mark, and Luke as his evangelistic predecessors, it should perhaps come as no surprise that he feels a certain diffidence even toward father *Jesus*. For if Jesus can say, "*I* am the truth," what is there left for his son John to say? The evangelist, in seeking to carve out a place for himself as the arbiter of all truth, finds that his place was originally filled by the Son of God, who necessarily left the world that John might succeed him: when Jesus is about to go to the Father, he tells his followers, "I go to prepare a place for you" (14:3)—but John senses that Jesus had *better* go, or there will be no place for a new son here on earth; if he stays, there will be no need for John and his Gospel. As Jesus put it, "He who believes in me will produce greater works than these *because* (!) I go to the Father" (14:12). According to John, Jesus joins the Father *in order that* he may be succeeded, and surpassed, by his true son. "For this is the will of my Father," says Jesus, "that every one who sees the Son and believes in him should have eternal life, and I will raise him up at the last day" (6:40)—raise *whom* up at the last day? Perhaps, every one who believes in the Son, come Judgment Day. More importantly, the "son" himself, John, the latter-day evangelist. And it appears from the syntax that the latter meaning is foremost in John's mind.

But when the Lord says, "I and the Father are one," he wields a blade that cuts both ways. His inheritance as the true Son resolves the problem of authority for his Gospel ("He who rejects me rejects my Father also"—15:23), but raises the question of whether his word is not merely an unnecessary repetition. Jesus as Son finds his authority in the Father, but must also confess "that the Father is greater than I" (14:28), for "the Son can do nothing of his own accord, but only what he sees the Father doing; for whatever he does, that the Son does in like manner" (5:19). Jesus knows that the son can at best hope to duplicate the glory of the renowned father, an insight which sometimes makes for a strangely difficult transition: "Truly, truly, I say to you," says Jesus, "he who receives whomever I send, receives *me*; and he who receives *me*, receives the *one who sent me*. Having said these things, Jesus was troubled in spirit" (13:20–21).

John has no conscious desire to be *greater* than Jesus, but neither does he wish to be a lesser son, or merely a belated repetition. He wants rather to make a significant and original contribution. John therefore shapes a role for himself as the son whose Gospel *completes* and *consummates* the life and work of the Son. His unique mission is subtly hinted at in his account of the crucifixion: Jesus was crucified not at the third hour, as in Mark, but at the sixth hour (Mark 15:25; John 19:14). "After this, Jesus, perceiving that all things were now complete, cried, 'I thirst!' " (19:28). This seemingly insignificant addition to the synoptic Gospels recalls the earlier scene in John when at the sixth hour Jesus required water (standing for the Baptist) before he could give the woman (Israel) the gift of the spirit. On that occasion Jesus said, "Whoever drinks of the water that I shall give him will never thirst" (4:14). But John suggests that it is now time for some fresh living water, for Jesus is thirsty. All he gets, however, is sour wine—which in Matthew, Mark, and Luke was merely sour wine but which here comes to stand for the synoptic Gospels themselves. The implication is that the new son must step forward with living water and new wine, for the Scripture, or *graphē*, will not be "made complete" until the true Logos (John's Gospel) is generated from above by the son and heir of the Son of God—so that John may truly say, "My food is to do the will of the one who sent me, and to *complete* his work" (4:34). The point is subtly underscored by earlier passages. At Cana, for example, there were only six pots of water, which, according to biblical numerology, is a sign of imperfection. John's Gospel, a pot of new wine, is the seventh. Similarly, the woman at the well had five lovers. Jesus appeared as the sixth, the spiritual bridegroom, but it is John, the seventh, who completes the tale. Again, the cripple at the Pool of Bethzatha waited as thirty-eight angels came and went. Jesus appeared as the thirty-ninth, but John, the fortieth, is the one who finally points the way to the promised land. It is therefore not until Jesus has named his spiritual heir that he can say, "It is finished" (19:30). "Then, bowing his head, he delivered up his spirit"—not to God in heaven, but to John.

All this might prompt us to ask of John what the Jews asked of Jesus: Are you greater than our father who died? (8:53). The answer is a qualified "No." In some ways, John does preempt the Son, as for example, in his account of Lazarus. Luke's Lazarus was not resurrected. John's is resurrected twice, as it were, and John's own miracle comes first: "For as the father raises the dead and gives them life, so also the son gives life to whom he will" (5:21). John wills to breathe life into Luke's Lazarus, so that Jesus may follow him in giving life to him as well. But John's "sign" is strictly a symbolic triumph; he knows that he has no power literally to raise men from the dead, or to preempt Jesus.

If John has any Oedipal designs on his spiritual father, he suppresses them. We may return again to the crucifixion scene: "Standing by the cross of Jesus were his mother and his mother's sister, Mary the wife of Clopas and Mary Magdalene," together with that disciple whom Jesus loved (19:25). The carefully balanced parallelism, with one "and" missing, raises the perennial question: Are there two women, or four? Is Jesus's mother the wife of "Clopas" ("renowned father"), and is Magdalene her sister? If not, who is this wife of a renowned father, mentioned nowhere but here, in the Fourth Gospel, and why is Jesus' beloved son standing beside her? Jesus may be disturbed by the same thought: for "when Jesus saw [his] mother and [the] disciple whom he loved standing near, he said to the mother, 'Woman, behold, your son!' Then said he to the disciple, 'Behold, your mother!' " (19:26–27) —as if to say, "Woman, remember, this man is not your husband," and "Son, you are not to be a 'renowned father,' but must remain a son."

John seems compelled to remind himself, time and again, that he is not, in fact, greater than his father, the Son: "You must *remember* the word which I spoke to you," says Jesus, "a servant is *not greater* than his lord" (15:20). But if "he who is sent is *not greater* than the one who sends him" (13:16), neither need he be any *less*. John resolves his ambiguous status as son by establishing finally a mystical union between himself and the Logos of God, so that he may partake of the Father's greatness without seeking to preempt the Son in any way:

> He who has seen me has seen the father. How do you say, "Show us the father"? Do you not believe that I am in the father and the father in me?
>
> (14:9–10)

Just as the Word and the Father are one, so is the Word one with John, and John one with the Father. The evangelist dares not seek priority to Jesus. What he seeks rather is a perfect union, a oneness with both Father and Son, that he may be with them "since the beginning." That John and Jesus talk alike, we have already seen; there is no distinction made between the language of one and that of the other. The implied identification, which is hardly accidental, is underscored by John's frequent use of Greek, puns on such words as *logos, sēmeion, ergon, anōthen,* and *akoloutheō.* Jesus' *sēmeia* ("signs") and John's *sēmeia* ("written proofs, letters") are inseparably one. Jesus' word (*ho logos autou*) and John's word *of* him (*ho logos autou*) are identical (4:41; 5:24, 38; 8:31, et al.). Jesus had "done one deed" (*hen ergon epoiēsa*), John has "written one work" (*hen ergon epoiēsa*), and the world marvels (7:21; cf. 9:34; 5:20, 36; 10:25–38; 14:10–12).

Jesus' metaphors likewise refer equally to himself and to that son with whom he is at one: "A woman giving birth is distressed," he says, "for her hour has come; but when she brings forth the child she no longer remembers her anguish, for joy that a child is born into the world" (16:21). But then the metaphor seems to get confused: "Now, then, *you* are distressed—but I will see you again, and your hearts will have joy, and no one will take your joy from you" (16:22). It's as if Jesus, whose hour has come (12:23; 13:1), must labor to produce a child to take his place in the world, that his joy may be full. The child in turn (specifically, John) must then give birth, not to a new child, but to a returning Jesus, that *his* joy may be full. The true Son, having vanished from the world, is to be brought back into the world through his child, John. Again, if "he who enters by the door is the shepherd of the sheep" (10:2), who is the door? Jesus says, "I am the door of the sheep" (10:8). Who, then, is the shepherd? Jesus and John are one door, one shepherd. Jesus is the door who admits John into the kingdom; John in turn is the door who brings the true Jesus back into the world, as in the metaphor of the woman in travail. Jesus is the shepherd who becomes the Lamb; John is a following lamb who becomes the shepherd, he in the father and the father in him. John serves the Son by following him; and the Son in turn serves John, serves him as a trope for *John himself*—perhaps the most audacious substitution in the history of our literature. John thus takes his place as the third member of an everlasting trinity: Father, Son, and the son of the Son. John is that logos from above which was in the beginning with God, and, in a sense, was God, from the first moment of creation.

The logos which creates all things is not, after all, that of the Father, but rather is that of the Son, at once the logos of Christ and the logos of John:

> This very logos was in the beginning with God: all things
> came into being through the logos, and without it there

came not one thing into the world. That which has come into being was life in the logos, and the life was the light of men.

(1:2–4)

Through John's eternally present, infinitely creative word, a whole world has come into being. He, along with God and the *P* writer of Genesis, creates through the power of the word itself: "Let there be light"—and there was light. His transcendent word is prior to all other beginnings, narrative or otherwise, prior to the synoptics, to the son of Zebedee, to John the Baptist, to the prophets, Moses, and Abraham. And there is a sense in which even the Father himself must follow the all-fathering word of John, for it is John's word which declares him. Without the logos, nothing of God may be known. John the evangelist, though belated, is the prime mover whose word establishes the world. Our only task, and the only requirement for us to enter the kingdom of John's heaven, is that we learn to follow.

Peter's Denial

René Girard

Jesus quotes the prophet Zechariah to his disciples in order to describe for them what the effect of the Passion will be: "I shall strike the shepherd and the sheep will be scattered" (Zech. 13:7; Mark 14:27). The dispersal takes place immediately after his arrest. The only one not to run away is Peter. He follows the procession at a distance and makes his way into the courtyard of the High Priest while Jesus is being brutally interrogated inside the palace. He manages to enter the court-yard through the auspices of someone familiar with the place, "another disciple" who joined him. The "other disciple" is not mentioned by name but is meant without a doubt to be the apostle John.

Mark tells us that Peter had followed Jesus at a distance, "right into the courtyard of the high priest; and he was sitting with the guards, and warming himself at the fire" (Mark 14:54). Nothing is more natural than this fire on a March evening in Jerusalem. "Now the servants and officers had made a charcoal fire, because it was cold, and they were standing and warming themselves; Peter also was with them, standing and warming himself" (John 18:18).

Peter is already doing what the others are doing, and for the same reasons. He is imitating the others, but there is nothing remarkable about this. It is cold and everyone is huddled around the fire. Peter joins them. At first we are not aware of what should be noticed. Yet the concrete details are all the more significant in a text that provides

From *The Scapegoat.* © 1986 by the Johns Hopkins University Press, Baltimore/London.

so few. Three of the four Gospels mention this fire. There must be a reason for this, and we should try to discover it in Mark's text, which is considered the most *primitive.*

While Peter is standing below in the courtyard one of the maids of the high priest arrives. Seeing Peter warming himself, she looks into his face and says:

> "You too were with Jesus, the man from Nazareth." But he denied it. "I do not know, I do not understand, what you are talking about," he said. And he went out into the forecourt. The servant girl saw him and again started telling the bystanders, "This fellow is one of them." But again he denied it. A little later the bystanders themselves said to Peter, "You are one of them for sure! Why, you are a Galilean." But he started calling down curses on himself and swearing, "I do not know the man you speak of." At that moment the cock crew for the second time, and Peter recalled how Jesus had said to him, "Before the cock crows twice, you will have disowned me three times." And he burst into tears.
>
> (Mark 14:66–72)

At first we think that Peter is a brazen liar. Peter's denial has forced him to that lie, but there is no such thing as a pure and simple lie, and this one, on second thought, is not that simple. What is actually being asked of Peter? He is being asked to admit that *he was with Jesus.* But since the recent arrest there are no longer disciples or community surrounding Jesus. Neither Peter nor anyone else is truly with Jesus any longer. As we know, existentialists recognize in "the being with" an important modality of being. Martin Heidegger calls it the *Mitsein,* which may be literally translated *the being with.*

Jesus' arrest seems to have destroyed any possible future *being with Jesus,* and Peter seems to have lost all memory of *having been.* He answers as if in a dream, like a man who does not really know where he is: *"I do not know, I do not understand, what you are talking about."* He may well not have understood. He is dispossessed and destitute, reduced to a vegetablelike existence, controlled by elemental reflexes. He feels cold and turns to the fire. Elbowing one's way to the fire and stretching hands toward it with the others is to act like one of them, as if one belongs with them. The simplest gestures have their logic, and that logic is as much sociological as biological, the more powerful because it is situated far beneath the level of consciousness.

All Peter wants is to warm himself with the others but, deprived of his *being with* by the collapse of his universe, he cannot warm himself without wanting obscurely the being that is shining there, in this fire, and the being that is indicated silently by all the eyes staring at him, by all the hands stretched toward the fire.

A fire in the night is much more than a source of heat and light. As soon as it is lit, people arrange themselves in a circle around it; they are no longer a mere crowd, each one alone with himself, they have become a community. Hands and faces are turned toward the fire and in turn are lit by it; it is like a god's benevolent response to a prayer addressed to him. Because everyone is facing the fire, they cannot avoid seeing each other; they can exchange looks and words; a place for communion and communication is established. Because of the fire vague new ways of *being with* become possible. For Peter, *the being with* is re-created but in a different place and with different partners.

Mark, Luke, and John mention this fire a second time, at the moment when, in Mark and Luke, the servant girl appears for the first time. The impression is that it is Peter's presence around the fire rather than in the courtyard that provokes her interference. *"She saw Peter warming himself there, stared at him and said, 'You too were with Jesus, the man from Nazareth.'"* Peter perhaps had pushed his way to the front, and there he was right by the fire, in full light, where everyone could see him. Peter, as always, has gone too far too fast. The fire enabled the servant girl to recognize him in the dark, but that is not its chief role. The servant does not fully understand what scandalizes her in Peter's attitude and forces her to speak to him so insolently, but the fire, in Mark, is certainly there for a purpose. The companion of the Nazarene is behaving as if he were among his own, as if he belonged around this fire. Without the fire the servant girl would not have been so indignant with Peter. The fire is much more than an ordinary background. The *being with* cannot become universal without losing its own value. That is why it is based on exclusions. The servant speaks only of the *being with Jesus,* but there is a second *being with* around the fire; this is what interests the servant girl, because it is hers; she knows how to defend its integrity; that is why she refuses Peter the right to warm himself by the fire.

John makes the servant girl the porter, the guardian of the entrance. She is the one who allows Peter to enter the courtyard on the recommendation of the other disciple. The servant girl in fact plays the role of guardian. The idea in itself is excellent, but it forces the evangelist to maintain that Peter is recognized straight off, before he even approaches the fire. So it is no longer by the light of this fire that the servant recognizes the intruder; it is no longer the intimate and ritual character of the scene that rouses her indignation. Moreover, in John, Peter is questioned a third time not by the whole band of servants but by an individual who is presented as a relative of the man whose ear Peter cut off (in a useless effort to defend Jesus by violence, at the time of arrest). John prefers the traditional interpretation that recognizes only one motive in Peter's denial: fear. Although fear, of course, should not be entirely excluded, it should not be considered to play a decisive role, and careful study of the four versions—not even John's—does not support such an interpretation, despite first appearances. If Peter were truly afraid for his life, as most commentators suggest, he would never have gone into the courtyard, especially if he had already been recognized. He would have felt threatened and left immediately.

On the summons of the servant girl the circle loses its fraternal character. Peter wants to hide himself from sight but the crowd presses around him. He stays too close to the center, and the servant can follow him easily with her eyes as he retreats to the entranceway. Once there, he hesitates and waits for the sequence of events. His conduct is not that of a man who is afraid. Peter moves away from the light and the heat because he senses obscurely what the servant is trying to do, but he does not leave. That is why she can repeat her accusation. She is trying not to terrorize Peter but to embarrass him and make him go away.

Seeing that Peter is not about to leave, the servant becomes involved and repeats her news a second time. She announces that Peter belongs to the group of disciples: "This man is one of them." The first time she said it directly to Peter, but she intended it for the people around him, those who were warming themselves at the fire, members of the community threatened by the invasion of a stranger. She wanted to mobilize them against the intrusion. The second time she speaks directly to them, and achieves the result she wants; the whole group turns on Peter: *"You are one of them for sure!"* Your *being with* is not here, it is with the Nazarene. In the exchange that follows it is Peter who raises his voice and begins *"calling down curses on himself and swearing."* If he were afraid for his life, or even for his freedom, he would have spoken less forcefully.

The superiority of Mark's text lies in the fact that he makes the same servant girl speak twice running, instead of putting the words in the mouths of others. His servant girl is more prominent. She shows initiative and stirs up the group. We would say today that she shows leadership qualities. But we should always be wary of psychologizing; it is not the servant's personality that interests Mark but rather the way in which she unleashes the group mechanism, the way she brings collective mimeticism into play.

As I pointed out, the first time she is trying to stir up a group made sluggish by the late hour and the heat of the fire. She wants them to follow her example, and when they do not, she is the first to follow it. Her lesson has no effect, so she repeats it a second time. Leaders know that they must treat those who follow them like children; they must always inspire imitation. The second example reinforces the effect of the first, and this time it works. All the bystanders repeat together: *"You are one of them for sure! Why, you are a Galilean."*

The mimeticism is not characteristic only of Mark; the denial scene is completely mimetic in all four Gospels, but in Mark the mechanism for releasing the mimeticism is more clearly defined, from the beginning, in the role of the fire and in that of the servant girl. Only Mark makes the servant repeat herself twice in order to prime the mimetic mechanism. She sets herself up as a model and, to make that model more effective, she is the first to imitate it; she emphasizes her own role of model and details mimetically what she expects from her companions.

The students repeat what their mistress tells them. The very words of the servant are repeated but with something extra which reveals wonderfully what is at work in the denial scene: *for you are a Galilean*. Illuminated in the first place by the fire, then revealed by his face, Peter is finally identified by his accent. Matthew, as he does so often, puts on the finishing touches by making Peter's persecutors say, "Your accent gives you away." All those who are legitimately warming themselves around the fire are from Jerusalem. That is where they are from. Peter has only spoken twice, and each time only a few words, but it is enough for his listeners to know without a doubt that he is a stranger, a scorned provincial, a Galilean. The person with the accent, any accent, is always the person who *is not from here*. Language is the surest indicator of the *being with*. This is why Heidegger and his colleagues attach such importance to the linguistic dimension of being. The specificity of national or even regional language is fundamental.

Everywhere it is said that the essential, in a text or even in a language, that which gives it its value, is untranslatable. The Gospels are seen as inessential because they are written in a cosmopolitan, debased Greek that is deprived of literary prestige. Moreover, they are perfectly translatable, and it is easy to forget what language one is reading them in provided one knows it, whether it is the original Greek, vulgar Latin, French, German, English, or Spanish. When one knows the Gospels, translating them into an unknown language is an excellent way of penetrating the intimacy of that language with as little loss as possible. The Gospels are all things to all people; they have no accent because they are all accents.

Peter is an adult, and he cannot change the way he speaks. He is unable to imitate precisely the accent of the capital. Possession of the desired *being with* is not just saying the same things as everyone else but saying them the same way. The slightest nuance of intonation can betray one. Language is a treacherous servant—or a too faithful one—that always reveals the true identity one tries to conceal.

A mimetic rivalry is unleashed between Peter and his interlocutors and at stake is the *being with* that dances in the flames. Peter tries desperately to "integrate himself," to prove the excellence of his imitation, but his antagonists turn unhesitatingly toward those aspects of cultural mimeticism that cannot be imitated, such as language buried in the unconscious regions of the psyche.

The more deeply rooted, "authentic," and ineradicable is the belonging, the more it is based on idioms that seem profound but are perhaps insignificant, idiocies in both the French and the Greek sense of *idion*, meaning "one's own." The more something becomes our own, the more in fact we belong to it; which does not mean that it is particularly "inexhaustible." In addition to language there is sexuality. John indicates that the servant girl is young, and this may be a significant detail.

We are all possessed of language and sex. Of course, but why always mention it in the tone of the possessed. Maybe we can do better. Peter understands clearly that he cannot deceive the world, and when he denies his master so fiercely, it is not to convince anyone but to sever the bonds that unite him to Jesus and to form others with those around him: *"But he started calling down curses on himself and swearing, 'I do not know the man you speak of.'"*

This is a truly religious bond—*religare*, to bind—and therefore Peter has recourse to curses—like Herod in his exorbitant offer to

Salome. His violence and angry gestures are aimed not at Peter's interlocutors but at Jesus himself. Peter makes Jesus his victim in order to stop being the sort of lesser victim that first the servant girl and then the whole group make him. What the crowd does to Peter he would like in turn to do to them but cannot. He is not strong enough to triumph through vengeance. So he tries to conciliate his enemies by allying himself with them against Jesus, by treating Jesus as they want and in front of them, exactly as they themselves treat him. In the eyes of these loyal servants Jesus must be a good-for-nothing since he has been arrested and questioned brutally. The best way to make friends in a hostile world is to espouse the enmities and adopt the others' enemies. What is said to these others, on such occasion, varies very little: "We are all of the same clan, we form one and the same group inasmuch as we have the same scapegoat."

No doubt there is fear at the origin of the denial, but there is also shame. Like Peter's arrogance somewhat earlier, shame is a mimetic sentiment, in fact the most mimetic of sentiments. To experience it I must look at myself through the eyes of whoever makes me feel ashamed. This requires intense imagination, which is the same as servile imitation. Imagine and imitate are in fact one and the same term. Peter is ashamed of this Jesus whom all the world despises, ashamed of the model he chose, and therefore ashamed of himself.

His desire to be accepted is intensified by the obstacles in the way. Peter is therefore ready to pay very dearly for the admission denied him by the servant and her friends, but the intensity of his desire is completely local and temporary, roused by the excitement of the game. This is one of those small acts of cowardice that everyone commits and no one remembers. We should not be surprised at Peter's petty betrayal of his master; we all do the same thing. What is astonishing is that the sacrificial structure of persecution remains intact in the denial scene and is transcribed as a whole just as accurately as in the murder of John the Baptist or in the Passion story.

Certain words of Matthew must be interpreted in the light of this structural identity; their legal significance is merely their appearance. What Jesus is really saying to people is the structural equivalent of all persecution behavior:

> You have learned how it was said to our ancestors: *You must not kill*; and if anyone does kill he must answer for it before the court. But I say this to you: anyone who is angry with

> his brother will answer for it before the court; if a man calls
> his brother "Fool" he will answer for it before the
> Sanhedrin; and if a man calls him "Renegade" he will an-
> swer for it in hell fire.
>
> (Matt. 5:21–22)

The best way not to be crucified, in the final analysis, is to do as everyone else and join in the crucifixion. The denial therefore is one episode of the Passion, a kind of eddy, a brief swirl in the vast current of mimeticism of the victim that carries everyone toward Golgotha.

The formidable power of the text is confirmed immediately in that its true significance cannot be ignored without repercussion, without reproducing the structure of denial itself. More often than not this ends in a "psychology of the prince of the Apostles." Determining someone's psychology is always to a certain degree a trial. Peter's ends in acquittal diluted with blame. Peter is not completely at fault, nor is he completely absolved. He cannot be counted on. He is changeable, impulsive, somewhat weak in character. In other words he is like Pilate, and Pilate is somewhat like Herod, who resembles anyone at all. Nothing is more monotonous or simplistic in the last analysis than this mimetic psychology of the Gospels. It may not be a psychology at all. From a distance it takes on the infinite variety of the world that is so amusing, engaging, and enriching. Close up, the same elements can be recognized in our own lives and are, to tell the truth, scarcely amusing.

Around the fire the usual religion, which is inevitably mixed with sacrifices, surfaces, in defense of language and the *lares*, the purity of the familial cult. Peter is naturally attracted by all this, just as we presumably are, since we reproach the biblical god for depriving us of it. Out of wickedness, we say. It takes real wickedness to reveal the dimension of persecution in this immemorial religion which still holds us under its sway by indescribable bonds. The Gospel is not gentle with persecutors, who are ashamed like ourselves. It unearths even in our most ordinary behavior today, around the fire, the ancient gesture of the Aztec sacrificers and witch hunters as they forced their victims into the flames.

Like all deserters, Peter demonstrates the sincerity of his conversion by blaming his old friends. We understand the moral implications of the denial, we must also understand the anthropological dimension. With his oaths and curses, Peter is inviting those who surround him to form a *conjuration*. Any group of men bound by oath forms the *conjuration*, but the term is applied most readily when the group unanimously adopts as their goal the death or loss of a prominent person. The word is equally applied to rites of demonic expulsion and to magical practices intended to counter magic.

The experience of innumerable rites of initiation consists of an act of violence, putting an animal to death, or sometimes even a man recognized as the adversary of the whole group. To achieve that belonging the initiate must transform the adversary into a victim. Peter resorts to oaths or religious formulas to endow his denial with its initiatory force among his persecutors.

If we are to interpret the denial accurately, we must take into account all that has gone before in the synoptics, especially in the two scenes in which it is directly prepared and indicated. These are the two chief announcements of the Passion by Jesus himself. The first time, Peter does not want to understand: "Heaven preserve you, Lord, this must not happen to you." His reaction is the same as that of all the disciples. Inevitable at the beginning the ideology of success dominates this little world. They argue over the best places in the kingdom of God. They are mobilized for the good cause. The whole community is in the grasp of mimetic desire and so is blind to the true nature of the revelation. Jesus is seen above all as the miracle worker, the great leader, the political chief.

The faith of the disciples is clothed in triumphant messianism. It is nonetheless real for all this. Peter has shown us this, but a part of him is still weighing the adventure he is about to experience in terms of worldly success. What is the sense of a commitment that only ends in failure, suffering, or death?

On this occasion Peter is severely reprimanded: "Get behind me, Satan! You are an obstacle in my path" [*you scandalize me*] (Matt. 16:23). When it is proved to Peter that he is wrong, he immediately changes direction and begins to run in the opposite direction at the same speed as before. At the second announcement of the Passion, only a few hours before the arrest, Peter does not react in the least as he did the first time. *"You will all lose faith in me this night"* [*be scandalized*]. Jesus said to them:

> At this, Peter said, "Though all lose faith in you, I will never lose faith." Jesus answered him, "I tell you solemnly, this very night before the cock crows, you will have disowned

me three times." Peter said to him, "Even if I have to die with you, I will never disown you." And all the disciples said the same.

(Matt. 26:33–36)

Peter's apparent conviction becomes one with the intensity of his mimeticism. The "argument" has been reversed since the first announcement, but the basis has not changed. It is the same with all the disciples, who always repeat what Peter says, since they are as mimetic as he. They imitate Jesus through the intermediary of Peter.

Jesus perceives that this zeal is heavy with the desertion that will follow. He understands that his worldly prestige will collapse with his arrest and he will no longer be the sort of model for his disciples that he has been until now. Every mimetic incitement comes from an individual or group that is hostile to his person or his message. The disciples, and particularly Peter, are too easily influenced not to be influenced yet again. The text of the Gospel has shown this in the passages I have discussed. The fact that the model is Jesus himself is unimportant so long as it is imitated out of a conquering greed which is always basically identical with the alienation of desire.

Peter's first about-face, admittedly, is not in itself blameworthy, but it is not exempt from mimetic desire, and Jesus clearly sees this. He sees in it the promise of another about-face, which can only take the form of a denial, given the catastrophe that is about to occur. Thus the denial can be rationally predicted. In foreseeing it as he does, Jesus is only outlining for the immediate future the consequences of what he has observed. Jesus, in other words, makes the same analysis as we do: he compares Peter's successive reactions to the announcement of the Passion in order to deduce his probable betrayal. The proof of this is that the prophesy of his denial is a direct answer to the second mimetic exhibition of Peter's, and the reader draws on the same details as Jesus does to form his opinion. If we understand mimetic desire we cannot fail to draw the same conclusions. We are therefore led to believe that the character called Jesus understands this desire in the sense that we understand it. This understanding reveals the rationality of the link between the elements of the sequence formed by the two announcements of the Passion, the prophesy of the denial, and the denial itself.

From Jesus' perspective mimetic desire is unquestionably involved, since he resorts to the term that designates this desire, *scandal*, every time he describes Peter's reactions, including the denial: *You will all*

In order to understand the value of scandal in explaining, therefore, all these sentences must be reorganized. They must be treated like pieces of a puzzle which is the mimetic theory itself, once the correct arrangement has been found. This is what I tried to show in *Des choses cachées*.

We are therefore dealing with an extraordinarily coherent unity that was never perceived by the exegetes because its components are muddled, and sometimes a little deformed, due to the authors' lack of control. When left to themselves these authors tell us vaguely that *Jesus knows what is in man,* but they explain this knowledge poorly. They have all the details in their hands, but these are disorganized and contaminated with miracles because the authors have only partial control over them.

There is an irreducible supernatural dimension to the Gospels that I do not wish to deny or denigrate. But because of this we should not refuse the means of comprehension now available to us which can only decrease the role of the miraculous if they are truly means of comprehension. The miraculous by definition is the unintelligible; it is not therefore the true work of the spirit according to the Gospel meaning. There is a greater miracle than the narrowly defined miracle and that is something becoming intelligible that was not so—mythological obscurity becoming transparent.

Confronted with the text of the Gospels, proponents and opponents alike only want to see the miracle and unequivocally condemn even the most legitimate effort to show that its role may be exaggerated. But rational suspicion is in no way contrary to the Gospels which themselves warn us against abuse of the miraculous. The rationality I am disclosing, the mimeticism of human relations, is too systematic in principle, too complex in its effects, and too visibly present, both in the "theoretical" passages on scandal and in the accounts entirely controlled by it, to be there by accident. Nevertheless this rationality was not completely devised or created by those who put it there. If they had understood it fully they would not have interposed between their readers and the scenes we have just read the coarse presence of the miraculous cock.

Under these circumstances the Gospels cannot be the product of a work that was purely within the effervescent milieu of the early Christians. At the text's origin there must have been someone outside the group, a higher intelligence that controlled the disciples and inspired their writings. As we succeed in reconstituting the mimetic theory in a kind of coming and going between the narratives and the theoretical passages, the words attributed to Jesus, we are disclosing the traces of that intelligence, not the reflections of the disciples.

The Gospel writers are the necessary intermediaries between ourselves and him whom they call Jesus. But in the example of Peter's denial, and in all of its antecedents, their insufficiency becomes a positive quality. It increases the credibility and power of the witness. The failure of the Gospel writers to understand certain things, together with their extreme accuracy in most cases, makes them somewhat passive intermediaries. Through their relative lack of comprehension we cannot help but think that we can attain directly a level of comprehension greater than theirs. We have the impression therefore of a communication without intermediaries. We gain this privilege not through an intrinsically superior intelligence but as the result of two thousand years of a history slowly fashioned by the Gospels themselves.

There is no need for this history to unfold according to the principles of conduct articulated by Jesus; it need not become a utopia before making accessible to us aspects of the Gospel text that were not accessible to the first disciples. It is sufficient that there has been a gradual but continual growth of awareness of the representation of persecutions by persecutors which continues to grow without, unfortunately, preventing us from engaging in persecution ourselves.

In those passages that suddenly become clear, the Gospel text is somewhat like a password communicated by go-betweens who are not included in the secret. Those of us who receive the password are all the more grateful because the messenger's ignorance guarantees the authenticity of the message. We have the joyous certainty that nothing essential can have been falsified. My image is not a good one, however, for if a sign is to become a password it is sufficient to modify its sense by a conventional decision, whereas here there is a whole collection of signs, formerly inert and colorless, that suddenly catch fire and shine with intelligence, without any preliminary convention. A festival of light is lit around us to celebrate the resurrection of a meaning that we did not even know was dead.

Chronology

TEXTUAL		HISTORICAL
	?	The Creation and the Flood
	1800 B.C.E.	The Patriarchs and the Sojourn in Egypt (ca. 1800–1250)
	1700 B.C.E.	
	1600 B.C.E.	
	1500 B.C.E.	
	1400 B.C.E.	
	1300 B.C.E.	
	1200 B.C.E.	The Exodus and the Conquest (ca. 1250–1200)
		Joshua (ca. 1200–1150)
		The Judges (ca. 1150–1025)
	1100 B.C.E.	The Monarchy (ca. 1025–930)
	1000 B.C.E.	
The J Source (ca. 950–900)		The Two Kingdoms (ca. 930–590)

TEXTUAL		HISTORICAL
	900 B.C.E.	
The E Source (ca. 850–800)		
	800 B.C.E.	
Amos, Proverbs 10–22:16 (ca. 750)		
Hosea (ca. 725)		The Fall of Samaria (ca. 720)
Micah, Proverbs 25–29, Isaiah 1–31, JE redaction (ca. 700)	700 B.C.E.	The Reformation of Josiah (ca. 700–600)
Deuteronomy, Zephaniah (ca. 650)		
Nahum, Proverbs 22: 17–24 (ca. 625)		
Deuteronomy–Kings (ca. 600–500), Jeremiah, Habakkuk (ca. 600)	600 B.C.E.	The Fall of Jerusalem and the Exile to Babylonia (ca. 587–538)
Job 3–31, 38–42:6 (ca. 575)		
Isaiah 40–55, Job 32–37 (ca. 550)		The Return (ca. 538)
Isaiah 56–66, Jeremiah 46–52, Ezekiel 1–37, 40–48, Lamentations (ca. 525)		
Job redaction, the P Source, Haggai, Zechariah 1–8, Jeremiah 30–31 (ca. 500)	500 B.C.E.	
Additions to Ezekiel 1–37, 40–48 (ca. 475–400)		Nehemiah and Ezra (ca. 475–350)
Joel, Malachi, Proverbs 30–31, Lists (ca. 450)		
JEP redaction [Genesis–Numbers], Isaiah 32–35, Proverbs 1–9, Ruth, Obadiah (ca. 425)		
JEPD redaction, Jonah, Psalms, Proverbs redaction, Song of Songs, Chronicles, Ezra, Nehemiah (ca. 400)	400 B.C.E.	The Hellenistic Period (ca. 363–330)
Ecclesiastes (ca. 350)		
Zechariah 9–14 (ca. 325)		

TEXTUAL		HISTORICAL
	300 B.C.E.	
Isaiah 24–27, Ezekiel 38–39 (ca. 300)		
The Septuagint, a translation of the Hebrew Bible into Greek (ca. 250–100)		
	200 B.C.E.	
		The Maccabean Revolt (ca. 165)
Daniel (ca. 175)		
Esther (ca. 100)	100 B.C.E.	
		Pompey takes Jerusalem (ca. 63)
	10 B.C.E.	
		Birth of Christ (ca. 6)
	B.C.E.	
	C.E.	
	C.E. 10	
	C.E. 20	
		Baptism of Christ and the beginning of John's Ministry (ca. 26)
	C.E. 30	Crucifixion of Christ and Pentecost (ca. 30)
		Conversion of Paul (ca. 32)
	C.E. 40	Martyrdom of James (ca. 44)
		Paul and Barnabas visit Jerusalem during famine (ca. 46)
		Paul's First Missionary Journey (ca. 47–48)
Galatians (ca. 49)		
Thessalonian Letters (ca. 50)	C.E. 50	Paul's Second Missionary Journey (ca. 49–52)

167

TEXTUAL	C.E.	HISTORICAL
Corinthian Letters (ca. 53–55) Romans (ca. 56)	C.E. 50	Paul's Third Missionary Journey (ca. 52–56) Paul is arrested in Jerusalem and is imprisoned by Caesar (ca. 56–58) Paul's voyage to Rome and shipwreck (ca. 58)
Philippians (ca. 60) Colossians, Philemon (ca. 61–62) Mark (65–67)	C.E. 60	First Roman imprisonment of Paul (ca. 59–60) Paul's release and last travels (ca. 61–63) Paul's second Roman imprisonment, martyrdom and death (ca. 64–65)
	C.E. 70	Death of Peter (ca. 64–65) Fall of Jerusalem (ca. 70)
Matthew (75–80)	C.E. 80	
Canonization of the Hebrew Bible at Synod of Jamnia (ca. 90) Ephesians, Hebrews, Revelation, Luke, Acts (ca. 95); 1 Peter (ca. 95–100), Fourth Gospel (ca. 95–115)	C.E. 90	Persecutions under Emperor Domitian discussed in Revelation (ca. 93–96)
	C.E. 100	
Johannine Epistles (ca. 110–115) James, Jude (ca. 125–150)	C.E. 125	
2 Peter (ca. 150) Timothy, Titus (ca. 160–175)	C.E. 150	

168

TEXTUAL

C.E. 175
C.E. 200
C.E. 300

C.E. 400

C.E. 500
C.E. 600
C.E. 700
C.E. 800
C.E. 900
C.E. 1000
C.E. 1100
C.E. 1200
C.E. 1300

C.E. 1400

C.E. 1500

Stabilization of the New Testament canon of twenty-seven books (ca. 350–400)

Jerome completes the Latin Vulgate, a translation of the Bible based on the Septuagint and translated from the Hebrew (ca. 400)

The first translation of the Bible into English, by John Wycliffe (ca. 1382)

The Gutenburg Bible is printed from movable type, ushering in the new era of printing (1456)

Erasmus finishes a translation of the Bible into Greek (1516)

TEXTUAL

Martin Luther translates the Bible into German (1522)	C.E. 1500
William Tyndale and Miles Coverdale's English translations of the Bible (1535)	
Matthew's Bible is produced, based on the Tyndale and Coverdale versions (1537)	
The Great Bible is produced by Coverdale (1539)	
The Geneva Bible, the first to separate chapters into verses (1560)	
The Douay-Rheims Bible, a Catholic translation from Latin into English (1582–1610)	C.E. 1600
The King James Version is completed (1611)	C.E. 1700
	C.E. 1800
The English Revised Version is coissued by English and American scholars (1885)	C.E. 1900
The American Standard Version (1901)	
The Moffatt Bible (1924)	
The Smith-Goodspeed Bible (1931)	
The Confraternity Version, an Episcopal revision of the Douay-Rheims Bible (1941)	
Knox's Version, based on the Latin Vulgate and authorized by the Catholic Church (1945–49)	
The Revised Standard Version (1952)	

TEXTUAL

C.E. 1900

The New English Bible, Protestant (1961)
The Jerusalem Bible, Catholic (1966)
The Modern Language Bible (1969)
The New American Bible, Catholic (1970)
Today's English Version (1976)
The New International Version (1978)
The New Jewish Version (1982)

Contributors

HAROLD BLOOM, Sterling Professor of the Humanities at Yale University, is the author of *The Anxiety of Influence, Poetry and Repression,* and many other volumes of literary criticism. His forthcoming study, *Freud: Transference and Authority,* attempts a full-scale reading of all of Freud's major writings. A MacArthur Prize Fellow, he is general editor of five series of literary criticism published by Chelsea House. During 1987–88, he served as Charles Eliot Norton Professor of Poetry at Harvard University.

A. C. CHARITY has been a Fellow of Trinity College, Cambridge, and Lecturer in English at the University of York. He is the author of *Events and Their Afterlife.*

HANS FREI is John A. Hoober Professor of Religious Studies at Yale University. He is the author of *The Identity of Jesus Christ* and *The Eclipse of Biblical Narrative.*

JEAN STAROBINSKI is Professor of French at the University of Geneva and the recipient of the 1984 Balzan Prize. A major contemporary critic of French literature, his works include *Jean-Jacques Rousseau: La transparence et l'obstacle, L'Oeil vivant, La Relation critique, 1789: Emblems of Reason,* and *Words upon Words: The Anagrams of Ferdinand de Saussure.*

LOUIS MARIN is Professor at the Ecole des Hautes Etudes in Paris and Visiting Professor at the Johns Hopkins University. He is the author of numerous books, among which are *Semiotique de la passion, Topiques et figures, Le Recit est un piege, La Critique du discours: Sur la "Logique" de Port-Royal et les "Pensees" de Pascal,* and *Utopics: Spatial Play.*

FRANK KERMODE is Professor of English at Columbia University. He is the author of *D. H. Lawrence, The Sense of an Ending, Forms of Attention,* and other works.

NORTHROP FRYE, University Professor Emeritus at the University of Toronto, is one of the major literary critics in the Western tradition. His major works are *The Anatomy of Criticism, The Critical Path: An Essay on the Social Context of Literary Criticism,* and *Fearful Symmetry: A Study of William Blake.*

ELISABETH SCHÜSSLER FIORENZA is Professor of New Testament and Theology at the University of Notre Dame. She is the author of *The Book of Revelation: Justice and Judgement, Bread Not Stone,* and *In Memory of Her.*

DONALD FOSTER is the author of numerous articles on the Bible.

RENÉ GIRARD is Andrew B. Hammond Professor of French Language and Literature at Stanford University. His works include *Deceit, Desire and the Novel; Violence and the Sacred;* and *To Double Business Bound.*

Bibliography

Achtemeier, P. J. "Mark as Interpreter of the Jesus Traditions." *Interpretation* 32 (1978): 387–99.

Banks, Robert, ed. *Reconciliation and Hope: New Testament Essays on Atonement and Eschatology*. Exeter: Paternoster Press, 1974.

Beardslee, William A. *Literary Criticism of the New Testament*. Philadelphia: Fortress Press, 1970.

———."Use of the Proverb in the Synoptic Gospels." *Interpretation* 24 (1970): 61–73.

Belo, Fernando. *A Materialist Reading of the Gospel of Mark*. Translated by M. J. O'Connel. Maryknoll, N.Y.: Orbis Books, 1981.

Best, Ernest. *Following Jesus: Discipleship in the Gospel of Mark*. Sheffield: JSOT Press, 1981.

Boring, M. Eugene. *Sayings of the Risen Jesus: Christian Prophecy in the Synoptic Tradition*. Cambridge: Cambridge University Press, 1982.

———. *Truly Human/Truly Divine: Christological Language and the Gospel Form*. St. Louis: CBP Press, 1984.

Brown, R. E. *The Gospel According to John*. Garden City, N.Y.: Anchor, 1970.

Brown, Raymond. *Community of the Beloved Disciple*. New York: Paulist Press, 1979.

Bultmann, Rudolf. *Theology of the New Testament*. New York: Scribner's, 1955.

———. *The History of the Synoptic Tradition*. Translated by John Marsh. New York: Harper & Row, 1968.

———. *The Gospel of John: A Commentary*. Translated by G. R. Beasly-Murray. Philadelphia: Westminster Press, 1971.

Caird, George. *Language and Imagery of the Bible*. Philadelphia: Westminster Press, 1980.

Carlston, Charles. *The Parables of the Triple Tradition*. Philadelphia: Fortress Press, 1975.

Cathpole, D. "The Fearful Silence of the Women at the Tomb: A Study in Markan Theology." *Journal of Theology for Southern Africa* 18 (1977): 3–10.

Chappuis, P. "Jesus and the Samaritan Woman: The Variable Geometry of Communication." *Ecumenical Review* 34 (1982): 8–34.

Conzelmann, Hans. "History and Theology in the Passion Narratives of the Synoptic Gospels." *Interpretation* 24 (1970): 178–97.

Corell, A. *Consummatum Est: Eschatology and Church in the Gospel of John*. London: Society for Promoting Christian Knowledge, 1968.

Crossan, John Dominic. *The Dark Interval: Toward a Theology of Story*. Niles, Ill.: Argus, 1975.

Culpepper, R. A. *The Johannine School*. SBL Diss. 26. Missoula, Mont.: Scholars, 1978.

Dahl, Nils A. *The Crucified Messiah and other Essays*. Minneapolis: Augsburg, 1974.

Dibelius, Martin. *From Tradition to Gospel*. New York: Scribner's, 1965.

Dodd, Charles H. *The Interpretation of the Fourth Gospel*. Cambridge: Cambridge University Press, 1960.

Donahue, John. "Jesus as the Parable of God in the Gospel of Mark." *Interpretation* 32 (1978): 369–86.

Findlay, J. N. "Thoughts on the Gnosis of John." *Religious Studies* 17 (1982): 441–50.

Fortna, Robert. *"The Gospel of Signs: A Reconstruction of the Narrative Source Underlying the Fourth Gospel*. Cambridge: Cambridge University Press, 1970.

Frei, Hans. *The Eclipse of Biblical Narrative: A Study in Eighteenth and Nineteenth Century Hermeneutics*. New Haven: Yale University Press, 1974.

Frye, Northrop. *The Great Code: The Bible and Literature*. New York: Harcourt, 1982.

Frye, R. M. "Literary Criticism and Gospel Criticism." *Theology Today* 36 (1979): 207–19.

Funk, Robert. *Language, Hermeneutic, and Word of God*. New York: Harper & Row, 1966.

Gill, J. H. "Jesus, Irony, and the New Quest." *Encounter* 41 (1980): 139–51.

Gruenler, Royce. *New Approaches to Jesus and the Gospels*. Grand Rapids: Baker Book House, 1982.

Haenchen, Ernest. *The Acts of the Apostles*. Philadelphia: Westminster Press, 1971.

———. *John: A Commentary on the Gospel of John*. Translated by R. W. Funk. Philadelphia: Fortress Press, 1984.

Hauerwas, Stanley. "The Moral Authority of Scripture: The Politics and Ethics of Remembering." *Interpretation* 34 (1980): 356–70.

Hawthorne, Gerald, ed. *Current Issues in Biblical and Patristic Interpretation*. Grand Rapids: Eerdmans, 1975.

Hick, John, ed. *The Myth of God Incarnate*. London: SCM Press, 1977.

Higgins, Angus. *The Son of Man in the Teaching of Jesus*. Cambridge: Cambridge University Press, 1980.

Kee, Howard C. *Understanding the New Testament*. Englewood Cliffs, N.J.: Prentice-Hall, 1973.

———. *Community of the New Age: Studies in Mark's Gospel*. Philadelphia: Westminster Press, 1977.

Kelber, Werner, ed. *The Passion in Mark*. Philadelphia: Fortress Press, 1976.

———. *The Oral and the Written Gospel*. Philadelphia: Fortress Press, 1983.

Keller, J. "Jesus and the Critics: A Logo-critical Analysis of the Marcan Confrontation." *Interpretation* 40 (1986): 29–38.

Kingsbury, J. D. *Matthew: Structure, Christology, Kingdom*. Philadelphia: Westminster Press, 1976.

Koester, Helmut. *Introduction to the New Testament*. 2 vols. Philadelphia: Fortress Press, 1982.

Kysar, R. *The Fourth Evangelist and His Gospel: An Examination of Contemporary Scholarship*. Minneapolis: Augsburg, 1975.

Meeks, Wayne A. *The Prophet King: Moses Traditions and the Johannine Christology*. Leiden, The Netherlands: E. J. Brill, 1967.

Minear, Paul S. "Gospel History: Celebration or Reconstruction." In *Jesus and Man's Hope*. Vol 2. Edited by D. G. Miller and D. Y. Hadidian, 13–27. Pittsburgh: Pittsburgh Theological Seminary, 1971.

Morgan, R. "Hermeneutical Significance of the Four Gospels." *Interpretation* 33 (1979): 376–88.

Nutall, A. D. *Overheard by God*. London: Methuen, 1980.

Painter, J. "Christology and the History of the Johannine Community in the Prologue of the Fourth Gospel." *New Testament Studies* 30 (1984): 460–74.

Perrin, Norman. *Jesus and the Language of the Kingdom: Symbol and Metaphor in New Testament Interpretation*. Philadelphia: Fortress Press, 1976.

Peterson, Norman. *Literary Criticism for New Testament Critics*. Philadelphia: Fortress Press, 1978.

———. "When Is the End Not the End?: Literary Reflections on the Ending of Mark's Narrative." *Interpretation* 34 (1980): 151–66.

Pregeant, Russell. *Christology beyond Dogma: Matthew's Christ in Process Hermeneutic*. Philadelphia: Fortress Press, 1978.

Reumann, John, ed. *Understanding the Sacred Text*. Valley Forge, Pa.: Judson Press, 1972.

Ricoeur, Paul. *Essays in Biblical Interpretation*. Philadelphia: Fortress Press, 1980.

Robinson, J. M. "On the Gattung of Mark (and John)." In *Jesus and Man's Hope*, 99–129. Pittsburgh: Pittsburgh Theological Seminary, 1970.

Robinson, James M., and Helmut Koester. *Trajectories through Early Christianity*. Philadelphia: Fortress Press, 1971.

Sandmel, Samuel. *Two Living Traditions*. Detroit: Wayne State University Press, 1972.

Schillebeeckx, Edward. *Jesus: An Experiment in Christology*. New York: Seabury Press, 1979.

———. *Christ: The Experience of Jesus as Lord*. New York: Seabury Press, 1980.

Schweizer, E. "The Portrayal of the Life of Faith in the Gospel of Mark." *Interpretation* 32 (1978): 387–99.

Segundo, Juan Luis. *The Liberation of Theology*. Translated by J. Drury. Maryknoll, N.Y.: Orbis Books, 1976.

Smith, D. Moody. *The Composition and Order of the Fourth Gospel*. New Haven: Yale University Press, 1965.

———. "Presentation of Jesus in the Fourth Gospel." *Interpretation* 31 (1977): 367–78.

Staley, J. "The Structure of John's Prologue: Its Implications for the Gospel's Narrative Structure." *Catholic Biblical Quarterly* 48 (1986): 241–63.

Sykes, S. W. "Story and Eucharist." *Interpretation* 37 (1983): 365–76.

Talbert, Charles H. *What Is a Gospel?: The Genre of the Canonical Gospels*. Philadelphia: Fortress Press, 1977.

Tannehill, Robert C. *The Sword of His Mouth*. SBL Semeia Supplements, 1. Philadelphia: Fortress Press, 1975.

————. "The Disciples in Mark: The Function of a Narrative Role." *Journal of Religion* 57 (1977): 386–405.

Tinsley, E. J. *The Imitation of God in Christ.* Philadelphia: Westminster Press, 1960.

Via, Dan O., Jr. *The Parables: Their Literary and Existential Dimension.* Philadelphia: Fortress Press, 1967.

————. *Kerygma and Comedy in the New Testament: A Structuralist Approach to Hermeneutics.* Philadelphia: Fortress Press, 1975.

Weeden, Theodore. *Mark: Traditions in Conflict.* Philadelphia: Fortress Press, 1971.

Wilder, A. N. "Myth and Dream in Christian Scripture." In *Myths, Dreams and Religion,* edited by J. Campbell. New York: Dutton, 1970.

Acknowledgments

"Introduction" (originally entitled " 'Before Moses Was, I Am': The Original and Belated Testaments") by Harold Bloom from *Notebooks in Cultural Analysis: An Annual Review*, Vol. 1, edited by Norman F. Cantor and Nathalia King, © 1984 by Duke University Press. Reprinted by permission.

"The Way of Jesus" (originally entitled "Jesus-Israel: The Way of Jesus") by A. C. Charity from *Events and Their Afterlife: The Dialectics of Christian Typology in the Bible and Dante* by A. C. Charity, © 1966 by Cambridge University Press. Reprinted by permission of Cambridge University Press.

"Jesus and God" by Hans Frei from *The Identity of Jesus Christ: The Hermeneutical Bases of Dogmatic Theology* by Hans Frei, © 1975 by Fortress Press. Reprinted by permission.

"A Struggle with Legion: A Literary Analysis of Mark 5:1–20" by Jean Starobinski from *New Literary History* 4, no. 2 (Winter 1973), © 1973 by *New Literary History*, University of Virginia. Reprinted by permission of the Johns Hopkins University Press.

"The Women at the Tomb: A Structural Analysis Essay of a Gospel Text" by Louis Marin from *The New Testament and Structuralism*, edited by Alfred M. Johnson, © 1976 by the Pickwick Press. Reprinted by permission.

"Hoti's Business: Why Are Narratives Obscure?" by Frank Kermode from *The Genesis of Secrecy* by Frank Kermode, © 1979 by Frank Kermode. Reprinted by permission of Harvard University Press, Cambridge, Massachusetts.

"Prophecy and the Gospel" (originally entitled "Sixth Phase: The Gospels") by Northrop Frye from *The Great Code: The Bible and Literature* by Northrop Frye, © 1981, 1982 by Northrop Frye. Reprinted by permission of Harcourt Brace Jovanovich, Inc., and Routledge & Kegan Paul Ltd.

"Women as Paradigms of True Discipleship" by Elisabeth Schüssler Fiorenza from *In Memory of Her: A Feminist Theological Reconstruction of Christian Origins* by Elisabeth Schüssler Fiorenza, © 1983 by Elisabeth Schüssler Fiorenza. Reprinted by permission of SCM Press Ltd. and Crossroad/Ungar/Continuum.

"John Come Lately: The Belated Evangelist" by Donald Foster from *The Bible and Narrative Tradition*, edited by Frank McConnell, © 1986 by Oxford University Press, Inc. Reprinted by permission.

179

Index

181